SOLDIERING AFTER THE VIETNAM WAR

SOLDIERING AFTER THE VIETNAM WAR

CHANGED SOLDIERS
IN A CHANGED COUNTRY

A MEMOIR

GLYN HAYNIE

Soldiering After the Vietnam War: Changed Soldiers in a Changed Country

For information about this title or to order other books
and/or electronic media, contact the publisher:

Glyn Haynie
www.glynhaynie.net
glyn@glynhaynie.com

ISBNs:
Hardback 978-0-9982095-5-5
Paperback 978-0-9982095-3-1
eBook 978-0-9982095-4-8

Printed in the United States of America

Cover Design, Interior Design, and Editing: 1106 Design, Phoenix, AZ
Author Photograph: Shannon Prothro Photography

John William, I love and miss you

CONTENTS

ACKNOWLEDGMENTS

Thanks to my brother John "Wayne" Haynie for contributing photographs and researching and providing information on our family members' military service and for verifying information about our assignments together.

Thank you to Dusty Rhoades, Dennis Stout, Jay Robinson, Chuck Council, Bruce Nugent, John Baxter, and Leslie Pressley for the photographs.

Thanks to Don Ayers for the photograph of the young soldier on the cover.

Special thanks to David Armstrong, John Felchak, Richard and Leah Kelly, and my wife, Sherrie, for helping me to get the book ready for publication.

Thank you, First Platoon, for being my brothers.

PROLOGUE

"Word to the Nation: Guard zealously your right to serve in the Armed Forces, for without them, there will be no other rights to guard."
— PRESIDENT JOHN F. KENNEDY

I enlisted in the Army July 28, 1968, and, after my infantry training, flew to Vietnam, March 10, 1969, at the age of 18, and my older brother, Wayne, 20 years old, sat next to me on the long flight to a foreign land and an unpopular war. Two weeks after my 19th birthday, Wayne left for Korea, and I went to serve with the First Platoon Company A 3rd Battalion/1st Infantry Regiment 11th Infantry Brigade Americal (23rd) Infantry Division. The First Platoon patrolled the area of the Quang Ngai Province in the Central Highlands of South Vietnam. We, as a platoon, survived fighting the North Vietnamese Army (NVA) and Vietcong, ambushes, sappers, and psychological operations, with the enemy telling us to surrender, leave, or get wiped out, while building a firebase.

During my one-year tour, I experienced many hardships, including the death of 13 platoon brothers and the wounding of 12, three of the 12 wounded more than once. The first time I repeated the names of the 13 killed was early morning of August 16, 1969. A squad member woke me because I was reciting the names out loud in my sleep, and he feared it might attract the enemy. The death of the 13 followed me the rest of my life. I wasn't haunted by them and didn't avoid their presence. I wanted them with me. I wanted to honor them and keep their memory alive. This wasn't a burden but a responsibility and honor I freely accepted. With this responsibility, my time in Vietnam wasn't forgotten, either. The 13 men who made the ultimate sacrifice for our country are Bruce Tufts, Juan Ramos, Eldon Reynolds, Jerry Ofstedahl, Robert Swindle, Richard Wellman, Paul Ponce, Joe Mitchell, James Anderson, Danny Carey, Gary Morris, Roger Kidwell, and Willmer Matson.

I thought I would never remember the details of my time in war 47 years ago, but all I had to do was sit in my office chair behind my computer and tap out one line on the keyboard to read on the screen. That's when I saw the details of the forgotten events of years past right in front of me, never thinking how painful it may be to go back to my days in Vietnam. Reading my book *When I Turned Nineteen: A Vietnam War Memoir*, you will have a better understanding of me, the young 19-year-old who returns home from an unpopular war and the influences, challenges, and decisions I faced after the war.

Inspired by a mixture of nostalgia and military service after the Vietnam War, I write of my journey as a United States Army Noncommissioned Officer and my yearning to see my brothers of First Platoon. Since memories can get lost in the clutter of time, I've attempted to share those 20 years of service as honestly as possible. The paths I took after coming home from war weren't predetermined but decided by events and how people I met along the way guided me on the decisions made. I'm sure fighting and surviving the Vietnam War influenced the decisions, too.

After doing the job my country sent me to do, I returned home to a country that had changed. The war in Vietnam was an unpopular war. Many Americans at home despised and vilified returning soldiers. There were few "Welcome Home" signs, cheers, or parades. Instead, often there were protestors. There was hate, name-calling, and disrespect. Young soldiers already impacted by their combat experiences in Vietnam now had to deal with the depression, anger, and resentment caused by their fellow countrymen. Some returning soldiers used alcohol or drugs, sometimes both, to deal with the aftermath of combat and war, and the treatment received after coming home.

Despite this, I continued to serve my country. Staying in the Army, I rose through the ranks: Squad Leader, Platoon Sergeant, Drill Sergeant, First Sergeant, finally becoming an instructor at the United States Army Sergeants Major Academy (USASMA) and retiring after 20 years of service.

My story isn't about war but of service to country and the consequences of that service for soldiers and their families. There are no claims that I had an extraordinary career, but my career did coincide with extraordinary times within the Army, and I met extraordinary soldiers, NCOs, and officers along the way. Soldiers today are experiencing far more hardships than I had, with their many deployments and separations from their families. They have my highest respect.

FORT BENNING, GEORGIA

"War is fear cloaked in courage."

— General William Westmoreland

March 7, 1970, I flew back from Cam Ranh Bay, South Vietnam, with a friend, Michael Smith, sitting next to me, stopping at Tokyo, Japan, and then at Anchorage, Alaska, and on to Seattle, Washington. Michael and I smiled once the wheels of the plane touched the Seattle runway. I knew we'd made it home and hadn't felt this happy in a year. Maybe I did leave the fear in Vietnam. We boarded buses to go to Fort Lewis. After we completed processing and left Fort Lewis for the Seattle airport, I said my goodbyes to Michael and boarded my flight for my first assignment at Fort Benning in Columbus, Georgia, my hometown. I planned on staying at my parents' home while on a 30-day leave before reporting for duty at Fort Benning. I still had 15 months left in the Army.

Fort Benning, named after Brigadier General Henry L. Benning, who served in the Confederate States Army, straddles the Alabama-Georgia border next to Columbus and is the Home of the Infantry. It was at Fort Benning where the 199th Light Infantry Brigade formed in 1966 for deployment to Vietnam. My father was the Adjutant General Officer (AG) when the brigade deployed to Vietnam.

The flight was uneventful, and, once we landed, I moved along the aisle to the front cabin door to exit. I followed the passengers into the waiting section, where my mother and father were waiting to greet me. I hugged my mother and then shook my father's hand. As we shook hands, I sensed he was proud of me, but he never said so. On the ride home, outside Atlanta, my dad asked if I was hungry, and I said, "Yes—a hamburger, fries, and a chocolate milkshake." He stopped, and I ordered my meal and ate it on the drive home; the meal tasted better than I remembered from a year earlier. The hour-long ride to Columbus went fast as we talked about Columbus, the Army, and my old friends. Arriving home, there were no bands, no parade, no one to welcome me home but my parents and my sister. Wayne was in Korea and wouldn't be home until early April.

Once home, I tried to reconnect with high school friends but found it difficult to reestablish the relationships I had before going to Vietnam. None of my friends had served yet; later, some would go to Vietnam. We no longer had much in common, and they were doing the same things we did as high school kids: sitting around the hamburger joint, burning rubber in the parking lot, flexing muscles, and flirting with the girls. And something new had developed during my absence—doing drugs. I didn't smoke grass or take any other drug while in Vietnam and don't recall being exposed to it. Trying to fit in, I indulged in taking drugs, mainly marijuana, but found alcohol my choice and stayed home more, drinking Jim Beam and Coke as soon as I got off work. I don't know if I drank or smoked grass because of the war or if it was normal to indulge every day, but I knew that, when I drank or smoked, I didn't think of Vietnam as much.

LIVING WITH FEAR

I came back home with no time to readjust to my earlier life after the exposure to hate, pain, stress, and fear—all the effects of war. I learned to hate the enemy. Hating the NVA and Vietcong became easy after they killed or wounded my platoon brothers, and hate made it easier to kill them. This hate remained for years after coming home. The sights, sounds, and smells of war still clung to me. There were no support groups to help me find my way back to civilization, which made me feel more isolated and unappreciated. It's not a parade I needed but to hear the words "Welcome Home" and to feel that those around me were *thankful* that I served our country during war—the gratitude that every generation before us had received. But this wasn't to be.

I heard and received the opposite of what I expected. The Vietnam War was a different and an unpopular war. It was the first war reported in detail by the media and viewed on the television screen without a filter, which influenced the American people about the war without listening to the men who were fighting in Vietnam. No one in the Army questioned me regarding the war and the impact it had on me or asked what I thought of my time in war. My friends didn't question where I'd been the last year, even though they knew. It was as if no one wanted to acknowledge I served in Vietnam, not even the Army. It wasn't a time when family or friends wanted to listen. My time in Vietnam didn't exist. I'm sure many Vietnam veterans felt the same in their transition from war to coming home. I believe the treatment we received coming home did nearly as much damage as the war did.

I didn't know if I had something wrong with me or not as I repeated the names of the 13 killed in Vietnam and replayed those events every day. I knew I had built-up anger, but I didn't know what to do with it or where it came from, and I regretted going home, leaving my brothers in the jungle. I felt guilty for those days walking into ambushes that killed seven and wounded eight of my brothers. The fear kept me from sleeping at night; I brought the fear home with me. The fear clung to me as a constant reminder of where I've been and wouldn't let go of me. I desperately wanted to be free of the fear.

What I called "fear" has a multitude of feelings, sights, sounds, and smells. I didn't want to be alone, but I wanted no one with me. I always checked a room before I entered. I hated to go into the forest, but, when I did, I walked at a slow pace, looking for booby traps and ambush sites. When driving along the highway, I looked for probable ambush sites. I let no one stand behind me, and I faced the door whenever possible. The dark scared me, terrified me. The sound of a helicopter overhead, the clanking of treaded construction equipment moving, loud thumps or something banging, firecrackers exploding and weapons firing startled me. The smells of Asians or oriental food and the smell of diesel or jet fuel burning put my body and mind on full alert. When I was sleeping, every unfamiliar sound alarmed me, and I jumped out of bed. And I had dreams—I mean, terrifying, real dreams. Whenever I faced one of these scenarios, I thought, *Who will die today?* It put me immediately back in Vietnam. I still have the fear today.

I didn't know what to do with my feelings and memories: the guilt, the anger, the dying, the wounded, the hardships, and the horror that war brings, but I found drinking or doing the occasional drug helped for the short term. Eventually, I realized that living with the memories of war would be too difficult, and, to the detriment to myself and my good health, I took these feelings and memories and stored them in a box in the recesses of my memory to keep hidden away, never to open. Repeating the names of my 13 brothers—Tufts, Ramos, Reynolds, Ofstedahl, Swindle, Wellman, Ponce, Mitchell, Anderson, Carey, Morris, Kidwell, and Matson—was the only ritual or memory I didn't store away. I owed them that; I made it my responsibility to carry their memory!

MOVING OUT

Within days of being home, a conflict started between my mother and me. She wanted to treat me as a teenager, not as a man, a soldier, or combat veteran. She asked where I was going when I was leaving the house and reminded me I needed to be home by 11:00 PM, my curfew when I was in high school. This wasn't her being concerned but keeping an eye on me as if I were a child. I moved out within a week of being home.

First, I needed a car. I asked my dad if he'd take me to buy a car, and he agreed. Dad drove me to the Chevrolet dealership where he'd purchased his new cars for the past ten years and introduced me to Mr. Horn, his salesman. Dad bought a new car every three years, so they knew him in the dealership. Having more than $2500 from my pay the last 18 months and the money I won from the poker games in Vietnam, I'd pay cash for the car I bought. I test-drove three used Camaros, the car I wanted, but dad pushed a 1968, low-mileage, light-blue with a white vinyl top, two-door Cutlass Supreme Oldsmobile powered by a 350 V8 engine. Yielding to my father's advice, I bought the Cutlass. Being only 19 years old, I needed dad to sign the paperwork for registration and title. If memory serves me correctly, I needed to be 21 to register a car in Georgia. I thanked my dad for his help and drove home in my first car, the proud owner of an Oldsmobile. After we got home, I cleaned up and headed to the hamburger joint, where all my friends were, to show off my new car. My Oldsmobile impressed most of my friends because they drove much older cars.

I found a roommate, Sonny Tate, taller than me and slender, still trying to gain back the weight he'd lost in Vietnam, with dark hair and an easy smile. A friend, Dee, introduced me to Sonny. He'd returned from Vietnam around the same time as I had, and I believe he served with the 101st Airborne Division and planned on getting into law enforcement in a year, when he'd completed his time in the Army. We rented a two-bedroom, two-bath mobile home 15 minutes from Fort Benning. For two strangers, we got along well. Sonny was an instructor for the Hand-to-Hand Combat subcommittee, and Fort Benning assigned me to the Basic Rifle Marksmanship (BRM) subcommittee. The men I worked with were infantry Noncommissioned Officers (NCO) and had served in Vietnam. Sonny joined me most evenings drinking, and I believe each of us shared around a half a fifth a day. Sonny didn't want drugs in the house, and that included marijuana. I respected his wishes and brought no drugs into the house. Drinking and smoking grass became a normal occurrence for me after my experiences in Vietnam.

The leading news story on our local television station each night was Lieutenant William Calley's trial at Fort Benning. Reports stated that

Figure 1–1 Me, age 19, the day I returned home from Vietnam, March 7, 1970, in the backyard of my parents' house. Photograph by my mother, Judy Haynie.

Calley's unit had killed as many as 500 villagers near the village of Son My, at a hamlet called My Lai. The Army charged Calley on September 5, 1969, and the Army court-martial convened November 17, 1970, eventually convicting him on March 29, 1971, of murdering 22 unarmed South Vietnamese civilians. I was in the same division and brigade, different battalion, as Calley, arriving one year after the massacre, and wore the Americal Division insignia on the right shoulder of my uniform when I came home. The Americal Division insignia has a blue background, representing the infantry, and four white stars, which symbolize the Southern Cross. Soldiers wore their unit-of-assignment insignia on the left shoulder and the unit in which they served in combat on the right shoulder of their uniforms.

My Lai was in the same province, Quang Ngai, that my platoon patrolled and where 13 of my platoon brothers died. It appeared that the Americal Division insignia that I proudly wore signified to the American public only that I was a "baby killer." To them, there was no distinction between Calley and others who served in the Americal

Division. Throughout my career, fellow officers, NCOs and soldiers kidded me about being a "baby killer" when they recognized the Americal Division insignia I wore. "Baby Killer" became a popular chant from protesters. When this story broke, the division, still in Vietnam, changed all signage from Americal Infantry Division to read "23rd Infantry Division." This was how damaging the name "Americal" reflected on the soldiers and the Army, all because of this one criminal, a Lieutenant.

After the local news, I watched the national nightly news showing the fighting in Vietnam and giving the number of Americans killed and wounded and the NVA body count. I always hoped I'd get a glimpse of the platoon members in my old unit. The news covered the anti-war protesters as they grew more vocal and more violent. "Baby Killer" was a popular slogan of theirs. When I met people, and they learned of my Vietnam service, I could see the fear in their eyes, and their voice reflected disappointment, as if telling a child, "You know, you shouldn't have done that." Most hated the war, and it appeared they hated the soldiers who fought the war. We were young boys sent to war who sacrificed our innocence to a war we didn't cause. We did what our country asked of us without question and returned home as men, maybe damaged men, and no longer the innocent boys we'd been.

Most of the NCOs I worked with were my age, and we tried to blend into the civilian community when leaving the post. In retrospect, I realized how lucky I'd been to get assigned to Fort Benning and Columbus, a military town. It wasn't popular to be a soldier, and, in particular, a soldier who'd fought in Vietnam. My assignment helped me to avoid some of the animosity toward the military because the NCOs I worked with and the people I'd gone to high school with isolated me from the general public.

RIFLE RANGE—FIRST ASSIGNMENT

The Army expected me to "look" professional, so I had to wear a heavily starched uniform, fatigues with creases in the trouser leg and the shirt sleeves, highly shined boots, and a military haircut. Putting on my trousers each morning became a chore. I had to push my foot through each leg of the trousers with enough force to "break the starch" of the uniform, and the same with the shirt sleeves, but I pushed my hand through the sleeve. The fly on the pants had buttons, not a zipper. The shirt was even more difficult. I had to loosen the starch around each buttonhole to get the button through the hole and considered myself lucky if the button didn't crumble in my hand. The buttons deteriorated over time because of the constant pressing and using starch. Walking in the uniform felt like being wrapped in cardboard, but I looked "professional."

I polished my boots, which the Army called a "spit shine," so they were a bright gloss, as was the black helmet liner I wore to identify me as cadre on the rifle range. I applied liquid floor wax on the toe and heel for an even, glossy shine, a trick I learned for the boots. The stateside uniform and dress code was far different from that for Vietnam. In Vietnam, we wore the same dirty, unkempt uniform for weeks and never shined our boots, and no one cared. We got haircuts as regularly as we could. Nobody complained much if our hair got too long. It took time for me to accept the "professional" look.

The Army required me to keep a military haircut, but I pushed this to the limit. I could blend in easier in the civilian community with longer hair. It was best for the least number of people to know I was a soldier. When in uniform, I used VO5 hair product to slick my hair down and back so it didn't appear as long as I kept it. I went to the same barber, Gene, as I did as a teenager, and he worked his magic to make my haircut look as if it met Army standards but left my hair longer than it should be.

I recall one instance when I removed my headgear and didn't have my hair slicked back. We were loading unused ammunition onto a truck, and a student, a young Second Lieutenant, around my age, looked up at me as he handed me an ammo box and said with as much authority as he could muster, "Sergeant, don't you think your hair is too long?"

"Lieutenant, when you go to Vietnam and come back home, you're allowed to grow your hair long," I replied with a big smile. We continued to load the ammunition, with no other conversation.

There were formations once a month, Headquarters Company, for payday, and we got off at noon. A formation consisted of all Company members and divided into four platoons of 40 men each. Most units held three formations a day for accountability and to pass out information. We were fortunate not to have the requirement of daily formations and had no other formations or physical training as a unit during the week. I don't believe I did physical training during my assignment at Fort Benning. I grew two inches but gained unnecessary pounds—too much drinking and junk food. I now stood five foot nine inches and 170 pounds, a big transformation from a year earlier when I'd left for Vietnam standing at five foot, seven inches and 135 pounds.

Being an assistant instructor, I showed how different weapons operated and fired. We taught rifle marksmanship with the M16 rifle. To show the evolution of weapons, I demonstrated firing the Browning M1918 BAR, M14 rifle, and the M16 rifle. For the demonstration, there were targets at various distances and balloons tied to the targets floating in the breeze. I had no problem hitting the targets or balloons with each of the rifles while firing at the targets using semi-automatic and automatic firing techniques.

The students, from the Infantry Officer Basic Course and other courses, filled the bleachers each morning to learn safety and the correct method for loading and firing the M16 and spent the rest of the day firing their weapons. We taught the students how to zero the weapon. To "zero the weapon" meant it fired accurately for the specific rifleman. The student would fire three to six rounds at a target 25 meters to his front. He adjusted his rear and/or front sight to move his shot group to the center of the target. Once the rifleman centered the three-round shot group, he'd zeroed his weapon. Now he could effectively fire his M16 at greater ranges with accuracy. The zeroing of the M16 shouldn't take more than 18 rounds.

I remembered the instructor calling me into the pit facing the bleachers full of students, where he instructed, and asked me to put the butt of the M16 against my balls and fire a round downrange. We'd rehearsed this in advance, and I feigned fear of hurting my manhood. We bantered back and forth for several minutes, until I took up the firing position with the butt of the rifle against my groin and the muzzle facing downrange. I exaggerated my fear while moving the selector switch to the semi-automatic position. Once off "safe," I waited for 5 seconds. I could hear everyone hold their breath; then I fired a round downrange, letting my groin take any recoil from the rifle. I knew the M16 wouldn't recoil enough to hurt me. The men in the bleachers let their breath out at the same time as I moved the selector switch to "safe." Then I turned to face the students, holding my balls, showing my manhood still intact. This act always received laughter and applause and eased the fear of the inexperienced riflemen that the weapon recoiling wouldn't be too much for them to handle.

When the students finished zeroing their weapons and qualifying, several weeks later, we assisted another range that was conducting a live fire and movement exercise. Each student, walking along an individual lane moving toward an "enemy" position, had an NCO attached to him. I grabbed the student's pistol belt at the small of his back with my right hand and the back of his collar with my left hand. Holding on with a death grip, I pushed him along the lane as he fired his weapon at targets. We, as safety NCOs, made sure he stayed even with the rest of the students to our left and right. The biggest fear was a student getting behind me and firing their weapon. I hated this training exercise.

Overall, I had an easy job; it wasn't stressful, but I normally worked a 10- to 12-hour day. We worked six days a week, a half day on Saturday, and we were off on Sunday. But it was still easier than working 24/7, as we had in Vietnam. The days we didn't have students, we maintained the range, which included cutting grass, painting wood surfaces, repairing and replacing targets, and refilling the sandbags that students used to support an M16 while firing at a target. I didn't like the sound of the M16s firing—it bothered me. I can't count the number of times I hit the ground when someone fired a weapon if I was not mentally prepared for it.

One morning, I walked into the range shack, a one-room white frame building built on a concrete pad, with two windows overlooking the range and a single wooden door. The furnishings were a metal gray desk with a gray office chair on four wheels, three or four gray metal folding chairs, and a black wood-burning stove with the smoke pipe running up the wall and through the ceiling, with a stack of wood next to the stove. The far back wall had a row of six metal gray wall lockers that we used to store equipment for the range. This was the range Noncommissioned Officer in Charge (NCOIC) office and where we gathered to drink coffee and bullshit until students arrived for training or after they left. I noticed a black NCO sitting by the stove, drinking coffee. He was wearing a crisp, pressed uniform with creases that looked as sharp as a knife blade and spit-shined boots in which I could see my own reflection. He was shorter than me, older, and had a solid build. The NCO looked up, and I saw the recognition in his eyes.

He said, "I see you made it back, Haynie; I must have done something right." That NCO, whom I'd met before, at basic training, had been my drill sergeant, Staff Sergeant Yulee.

After the initial shock, I said: "Yes dril- Yes, I did!" It surprised me he even remembered me. Now my drill sergeant and I are fellow NCOs and equals! I don't think he thought so. Even a year later, he instilled fear and awe as my drill sergeant.

One Saturday evening, Michael Smith telephoned me and wanted to visit. I hadn't heard from Michael since we'd flown home together from Vietnam. I cleared it with Sonny, and we made the sofa into a bed for him and had him share my bathroom. Michael flew in from Boston for a three-day weekend, and I picked him up at the Columbus airport, happy to see him again. He looked good and had gained weight. I don't recall what type of work he currently did or if he went to college. We drank and talked more about our time in Vietnam than we did any other topic. He wanted someone to talk to who'd shared the same experiences as he had, and I believed this to be the main purpose of his visit. Again, I felt lucky to be around soldiers. Even though, at work, we didn't talk of our time in Vietnam, it comforted me to be with soldiers who'd been there. We understood each other. The three days passed quickly, and it was time for Michael to return to Boston. We never saw each other again. Not keeping up with the soldiers I'd served with became normal for me, and I don't know why.

WAYNE COMES HOME

In April 1970, Wayne, my brother, came home from Korea, a happy day. When he'd reported to Korea, the replacement detachment stationed him at Camp Casey, in the Demilitarized Zone (DMZ), with the 7th Infantry Division. The mission of the 7th Infantry Division deters aggression and maintains peace on the Korean Peninsula. I hadn't seen Wayne since May 1969, when he left for Korea and I went to my infantry platoon in Vietnam. The Army discharged him when he came home. I introduced him to a friend I met after coming home, Dee, and they married within five months of starting dating. On November 17, 1971 at Fort Benning's Martin Army Hospital, Dee delivered Traci, their new daughter. I've never seen Wayne so excited.

Wayne bought a used Volkswagen Beetle after he returned from Korea. One day he stopped by where Sonny and I lived for a visit. The three of us were sitting around talking when we smelled smoke. We ran outside to see what was causing the smell and saw the small frame house in front of our place on fire. We grabbed the hoses connected to the front and rear spigots of the burning house and used these to try to put out the fire. As I ran around to the back of the house, I stepped into a pothole and heard a loud snap. I fell to the ground, letting out a low moan of pain. Wayne ran over and helped me into my house. The fire department soon arrived and finished putting out the fire. It was fortunate that the firemen found no one home. Wayne checked my ankle and saw it swollen three times its original size and turning black and blue. I thought, *What a bitch! I went a whole year in Vietnam without breaking a bone. Now, I'm home two months and break my ankle.* Wayne told me we needed to go to the hospital.

Wayne put me on the passenger side of my car, jumped into the driver's seat, and sped along Victory drive, the main road to Fort Benning

Figure 1–3 Left to right—Wayne Haynie and I standing outside our hooch at the Combat Center at the American Division firebase in Chu Lai, April 1969. This photograph was taken weeks before I joined my infantry platoon and Wayne went to Korea.

Figure 1–2 Left to right—I and Wayne Haynie standing outside our home, leaving for Vietnam, March 10, 1969.

Figure 1–4 Left to right—Wayne Haynie, with me picking Wayne up, returning from Korea, at the Atlanta airport, April 1970.

13

and Martin Army Hospital. He pushed the accelerator to the floor, and, as we increased speed, I shouted for him to slow down. Hearing a siren, I turned in the seat to look out the rear window and saw flashing lights. I told Wayne to pull over—that a cop was behind us. Wayne slowed and then pulled over, stopping the car. The policeman walked over to the car and peered into the driver's-side window. Wayne rolled the window down and shouted at the officer that I'd broken my leg and needed immediate medical attention. The officer looked at me and, without hesitation, said, "Follow me." When the officer said, "Follow me," I imagined that I looked worse than I felt.

Wayne pulled out onto the highway and followed the police car, with its flashing lights and siren blaring to the hospital for a sprained ankle. As we approached Fort Benning's main gate, the military police stationed at the gate waved us through. I guessed the police officer had called ahead. We pulled into the emergency room parking lot, and Wayne got me out of the car. While walking into the emergency room, with Wayne supporting me, we told the police officer thanks for his help in getting us to the hospital. With a smile, he waved and drove out of the parking lot, heading for Columbus.

Once in the emergency room at Martin Army Hospital, we sat in two of the chairs that lined the far wall in the emergency room waiting area. Wayne got impatient that no one was seeing me immediately and demanded that the orderly at the desk find a doctor to attend to my injury. He approached every medical person in the emergency room, demanding that someone look at my injury. I felt my face flush with embarrassment and thought it a good thing we hadn't served in my infantry platoon together in Vietnam. There was no telling what he'd have done if the enemy had wounded me or I'd had an injury. Wayne had always been overprotective of me when we were kids.

Growing up, Wayne and I were close. Our father was a career Army officer, and we moved many times during our childhood years. I believe moving and the military lifestyle made us even closer than most brothers. We attended school together (sometimes the same classroom), played Little League on opposing teams, and got into trouble together.

While sitting and waiting, I reflected on the last time I was at a hospital. It was August 20, 1969, after I received a Traumatic Brain Injury (TBI) from a command-detonated bomb on August 15, 1969. The only similarities were the Army uniforms, scrubs, and the smells of disinfectants. Sometimes I heard a low moan of pain or saw a patient with a wound that was bleeding heavily, and my mind wandered to the seven platoon members the blast wounded and the four who were killed that day.

After waiting for several hours, the doctor took x-rays, put a cast on my foot that extended over my calf, and gave me crutches. He said it was the worst sprain he'd ever seen and told me to come back in six weeks so he could remove the cast. I hobbled along with my new crutches, trying to keep up with Wayne as we walked to the car. Once we got to the car, I opened the passenger door, flung my crutches onto the back seat, and swung myself into the front passenger seat, making sure I didn't bump my left leg. I reminded Wayne there was no need to speed. On the way home, Wayne and I talked and laughed about the police escort we received to the hospital and how lucky he was not to have gotten a speeding ticket.

A week later Wayne came to my house and picked me up to go to our parents' home for dinner. On the way, we drove along Buena Vista drive, speeding past our childhood home, heading toward the back gate of Fort Benning. As Wayne drove, I rolled a joint and then flipped open my Zippo lighter, the same one I used in Vietnam, and lit the end of the tightly rolled joint. I took a deep drag, inhaled the harsh smoke, held it for several seconds, and then exhaled. I passed the joint to Wayne, and he, too, inhaled the harsh smoke and exhaled. We passed it back and forth, taking turns inhaling the drug of the marijuana cigarette. We talked about our youth and his time in Korea, and we laughed like two youngsters.

Wayne stopped laughing, sniffed the air, and said, "There's something burning, and it's not the joint or our cigarette smoke."

I told him that there was no smoke coming from the front. I looked around toward the rear of the car. Wayne looked in the rearview mirror he yelled, "Oh, shit! The car is on fire!" I saw black smoke billowing from the engine compartment. We pulled over, and Wayne opened the rear hood of the engine compartment and made sure there were no flames. He couldn't understand why smoke was pouring from the engine.

We were out in the boonies but, fortunately, near the last store, Taylor's Grocery Store, before entering a back gate to Fort Benning. Wayne pulled the car into the parking lot of the small grocery store and parked the car as smoke drifted out of the rear compartment. He opened his car door, ran to the back of the car, and opened the rear hood again to check the smoke. He determined he had a burned-out engine. I went inside to call mom to tell her we needed a ride home, and she arrived 20 minutes later. Wayne and I laughed during the ride home; my mom didn't understand the humor. I don't think we did, either. Wayne never smoked grass again after this happened. I believe he blamed the motor burning on our being high. And he got angry at the cost of repairing his car.

Wayne had several jobs but didn't find a job that held his interest, so he reenlisted in the Army. When discharged from the Army, he held the rank of Sergeant, but the Army enlistment standards allowed him to come back in a lower rank, Specialist 4th Class. As soon as he re-enlisted, he got orders for Vietnam. When Wayne told me he'd received orders for Vietnam, he asked to borrow my peace sign. Paul Ponce had given me the peace sign in Vietnam, May 1969, before being killed August 15, 1969. Wayne knew I wore the necklace as my good-luck charm, and I valued it because Paul gave me the peace sign. Wayne figured if it got me home, it would do the same for him. I gave the peace sign to Wayne but made him promise not to lose it and to bring it back. The Army canceled his orders two weeks before he had to report, and he remained at Fort Benning. I got my good-luck charm back. This gave me the opportunity to remind Wayne how lucky the peace sign was and the power it had. It got him out of going to Vietnam.

Thank you, Paul Ponce.

REENLISTING

Within two months, I met a young woman, Paula, who attended a party that Sonny and I hosted. She was attractive, with dark-brown eyes, slim and not too tall, with straight, dark-brown hair that flowed below her shoulders. We'd attended the same high school, but I didn't know her; I did know her older brother. Seven months later, we married, and, shortly after, she told me I'd be a father. After getting married, we found our own place to live—a small, white frame house around 900 square feet with two bedrooms, living room, eat-in kitchen, and one bath. It rented for $120 a month, and we had to pay utilities. We lived not too far from our parents' homes and had weekend meals with them. The four of us, Wayne, Dee, Paula, and I spent plenty of time together during the year 1971. Not long after we married, I bought my Camaro, yellow with a black vinyl top, three speed on the floor, with a 302 V8 engine and oversized tires on the rear, mounted on mag wheels.

My last three months of service I attended training the Army called "Project Transition" for Data Processing. "Project Transition" was a program to help soldiers leaving the Army gain a skill. The training programs offered were in such fields as automobile repair, electronics assembly, bookkeeping, drafting, masonry, phone repair, and data processing.

I learned how to do basic programming using Binary Code, which, for me, was the hardest part of the course. A large, warm room filled with mechanical and electronic sounds housed all the mystical computer equipment. The computers were large, bulky, strange-looking devices. Punch cards were the primary source of input, output, and storage that a computer fed into another computer, programming it for a specific task, and the output printed to a punch card or a printer. This course had challenges, but I made it through, and it fostered my interest in computers, which has lasted to this day. Not bad for a kid who had to go to summer school to graduate from high school.

But I reenlisted in June 1971 due to the baby coming and the lack of job opportunities. Heck, they were paying a $10,000 bonus before the Internal Revenue Service (IRS) took $2,000 in taxes, and we received a pay raise. With pay and allowances in 1971 at a pay grade of E5, I earned around $400 a month minus taxes. I reenlisted for six years—no big ceremony: just me and the Company executive officer, whom I'd met the day before and who administered the oath of enlistment. After the oath, I signed the paperwork and drove to finance to get my reenlistment bonus. Finance gave me $8000 in cash, eight bundles of $1000 each—fifty $20 bills. I stuffed the money into my uniform shirt because I didn't have a bag or briefcase to carry the money. I left finance, drove to my bank, walked in, pulled the eight bundles from inside my shirt, and stacked them on the counter to deposit into my account. The teller didn't appear surprised at the bundles of twenties and deposited the cash into my account. She must have handled many transactions like mine—soldiers depositing their bonus money—over the years.

The Army required a physical when reenlisting, and the reenlistment NCO scheduled my appointment. I showed up on time at the unit clinic and found 30 other soldiers waiting. The orderly told us to undress and wear only our underclothes. We entered a room one by one, carrying our uniforms, and tested for eyesight, hearing, heart, and lungs. The doctor poked and prodded every part of our bodies. At one of the last stations, an orderly instructed me to sit at a table, and he sat on the other side. He opened a book, placed it in front of me, and told me to read the numbers on each page.

Looking at the first page and then the second page, I saw no numbers at all. I thought, *Oh, shit. It's a psychological test to see if I'm screwed up from the war or maybe my TBI had something to do with me not seeing the numbers.* I pushed the book hard; it slid across the table and hit the orderly in the chest. He appeared surprised by my action.

As the orderly rubbed his chest he asked, "Don't you see any numbers?"

"I'm not taking a psychological test!" I snapped.

While laughing, he said, "The pages test to see if you can see colors."

What a relief! And I finally learned I had red-green color blindness. All these years I thought I didn't know my colors.

At the time of reenlistment, I didn't plan on making the Army a career. But I understood that I was making a big commitment when I reenlisted. We used the bonus money to pay off our cars—the Camaro and Paula's car, a Volkswagen Beetle. We rented a larger house and bought new furniture and appliances. The house was only a short walk or drive from Wayne and Dee and Dee's mother's house. The rest went into savings.

Tuesday, July 20, 1971, I took Paula to Martin Army Hospital at Fort Benning, and she gave birth to David. The nurse came into the father's waiting room and told me I had a healthy baby boy; I was excited and scared at the same time. The nurse continued and said David was underweight and jaundiced, and had to stay in the hospital for several days to gain weight and cure his jaundice. We found it hard leaving him there alone, but the doctor reassured us he would be fine. After David came into my life, I reduced my drinking to the weekends and seldom smoked pot. I became a proud father.

As I had less time remaining in the Army, before I reenlisted, the range Officer In Charge (OIC) assigned me to other duties. At one point, I drove a truck delivering ammunition needed each day or night to the ranges. Several months after I reenlisted, they assigned me as the Colonel's driver. Lieutenant Colonel Greer managed the ranges, and he cut the military figure: a tall, slender man in his late forties, with gray hair and a tan, weathered face. He had fought in WWII, Korea, and Vietnam. He appeared a kind and soft-spoken man and treated me well.

Most days, I drove the jeep into the woods so the Colonel could look for deer to hunt later and to find a place to safely trap shoot. A Captain rode with us most days, and the Colonel had him manage the mechanical device that flung the clay pigeons into the air while we shot them. He always brought an extra shotgun and had me shoot with him. I thought it sad having the Captain work the device for me and him seldom getting to fire at the clay pigeons, but it didn't appeared he cared.

I recall one day I came to work so tired because David stayed up crying night after night. I couldn't stay awake while driving and almost fell asleep at the wheel. The Colonel knew of David's crying and me not getting enough sleep, so he had the Captain drive that day while I slept in the back seat. The Captain said nothing. Several leadership traits I learned from Lieutenant Colonel Greer were kindness, compassion, and "Know your people and look out for their welfare."

Several days later, Paula and I took David to the emergency room. The doctor said he suspected meningitis, and he would need to do a spinal tap. He asked if I wanted to be with David during the procedure. I couldn't watch a large needle go into his back, so I declined. The test came back positive that he had meningitis, confirming the doctor's diagnosis. The doctor kept him in the hospital at Fort Benning for a week for a treatment with antibiotics; David was only three months old. He made a full recovery, much to our relief. I discovered parenting to be hard work but rewarding.

In September of 1971, I received orders for Germany and a reporting date of January 17, 1972. The career soldiers told me that, if I wanted to soldier, Germany is where to go. I looked forward to my new assignment and being with troops again in an infantry platoon. Still not having any formal leadership training was my only apprehension. Leading in the stateside army differed from leadership responsibilities in my platoon while in Vietnam. Staff Sergeant Yulee told me to attend the 7th Army NCO Academy in Bad Tolz once I got to my unit in Germany.

Not long after I received orders for Germany, Lieutenant Colonel Greer recommended me for promotion to Staff Sergeant, a pay grade of E6. I studied and appeared before the local promotion board. I did well, and my name was added to the promotion list. The promotion board was made up of four or five senior NCOs who asked technical questions on my Military Occupation Specialty (MOS), Infantry (11B). I expected my promotion to Staff Sergeant the next month, but shortly after I was put on the list, the Department of Army froze E6 promotions while they overhauled the promotion system. This freeze lasted more than a year. Just my luck!

January 1972—I'm 21 years old, married, one child, and leaving for my third assignment, second overseas assignment, after three years and five months of service.

CHAPTER 2

HEILBRONN, GERMANY

"We must learn to live together as brothers or perish together as fools."
— DR. MARTIN LUTHER KING, JR.

On a brisk mid-January Friday morning, I woke early, as I normally did, and, while staring at the ceiling, I repeated the names: "Tufts, Ramos, Reynolds, Ofstedahl, Swindle, Wellman, Ponce, Mitchell, Anderson, Carey, Morris, Kidwell, and Matson," and the face of each appeared as I said their name. I thought of my upcoming flight to Germany, and my body tingled with excitement—but also with apprehension: I wanted to go, but I didn't. I rolled out of bed to get ready.

Paula took me to the Columbus airport, and we said our goodbyes. I held and kissed David goodbye and then boarded a commercial flight, dressed in my Dress Green uniform, to Frankfurt in the central part of Germany, with one stop in London to refuel. As the airplane took to the air, I looked at the seat next to me and thought of Wayne sitting next to me on our flight to Vietnam. On this flight, I was alone, but I knew I wasn't going to war. I left Paula and David in Columbus with her mother, Nell, and they would fly to Germany once I settled in with the new unit and found housing for the family. We sold the Volkswagen and parked the Camaro at Nell's house.

NEW UNIT AND MISSION

Once the plane landed in Frankfurt, I departed the airplane and found the Army troop-replacement desk in the terminal, with a Sergeant manning it. The Sergeant scheduled transportation to the replacement center for new soldiers reporting to Germany. Along with a group of soldiers, I boarded an older green Army bus, with smoke pouring out of the exhaust and engine roaring, deafening any conversation on the bus. We drove to the replacement center, close to the airport. I stayed at the replacement center for several hours before the Company NCOIC loaded me and half the waiting group on another bus, many years newer than the last bus, for the trip to the 2nd Battalion/4th Infantry Regiment Headquarters Company in Stuttgart, my new assignment. The 56th Artillery Brigade, headquartered in Schwäbisch Gmünd, had my infantry battalion assigned to it. Schwäbisch Gmünd and Stuttgart were both in the southwestern part of Germany. Stuttgart is the capital of Germany's Baden-Württemberg state. The 7th Army had the 56th Artillery Brigade assigned to it. We wore the 56th Artillery Brigade insignia on our left shoulder sleeve to signify our assigned unit.

The bus maneuvered, winding along the narrow roads through town and then pulled onto the Autobahn, the federal controlled-access highway system in Germany, a new experience. There is no speed limit, except for construction sites, and the road signs looked strange. I wasn't positive I understood what most of the signs meant; some were obvious. Later I learned the meaning of each road sign so I could pass the international driver's test. All soldiers and family members driving in Europe needed an international driver's license.

When cars pulled up behind a slower-moving car, they flashed bright lights on and off several times, which meant "Get the hell out of the way and let the car pass." Flashing the car bright lights didn't mean the driver was aggressive; to the German driver, it was a courtesy to let the car pass. The car moved to the lane on the right and allowed the speeding car to pass.

We drove by towns and villages which looked old, interesting, and quiet. Most of the buildings were shops, churches, apartment buildings, or farmhouses and farm buildings. Seldom did I see single-family homes, and gray appeared to be a popular color. I was amazed at the abundance of fields being farmed in the countryside. I thought Germany, being an old country, would've had buildings everywhere and not as much farmland. My thoughts wandered elsewhere, to *Here I am, less than two years later, in another foreign country with a different language and customs, but much more civilized than Vietnam.*

Once the bus arrived at the Battalion Headquarters, along with the small group of soldiers, I stepped off the bus into the freezing afternoon air and reported to the Charge of Quarters (CQ) for instructions. We remained there for two nights, sleeping in a converted attic that accommodated ten bunks, with wall lockers to secure luggage. The attic space was large and clean but sparsely furnished, with only the ten bunks, the wall lockers, and one small game table with four chairs.

I bunked next to a Sergeant, Vaydon Jacobs, and we received the same unit assignment, Charlie Company. Vaydon, an American Indian from North Carolina, had dark hair and a complexion darker than mine. He was my height and had a solid build and an easygoing personality. We'd been in the Army the same number of years, and he'd served in H-Troop 17th Calvary in Vietnam, a unit that supported the 198th Infantry Brigade in the Americal Division. H-Troop worked the area across the river from my Company while I was in Vietnam. We served in Vietnam around the same time and became friends while in Germany.

Monday morning, before we left for the Company, the Battalion Commander and Command Sergeant Major, who had both served in Vietnam, talked to us regarding the Battalion mission. The Battalion Commander was black, six foot tall, with a slender build; he appeared too young for the rank he held. The Command Sergeant Major, a short man carrying extra weight, looked old and wore a buzz-cut-style haircut. As we walked out the front door of the headquarters building, the freezing air was the first thing I noticed. I disliked cold weather.

Vaydon and I threw our duffle bags into the back of the truck. We climbed into the canvas-covered rear of the 2½ ton truck and sat next to each other on the long bench that ran along the side of the truck. The driver started the engine and jerked forward to begin the trip to our infantry unit, Charlie Company 2nd Battalion/4th Infantry Regiment in Heilbronn, about halfway between Stuttgart and Frankfurt. During the ride, I thought of the last time I'd ridden in the back of a 2½ ton truck. It was less than three years ago, and I was reporting to Alpha Company on the firebase Charlie Brown. This ride contrasted the trip to Charlie Brown; I wasn't going into combat when I joined my unit. After a 30-minute freezing and uncomfortable ride north, Stuttgart to Heilbronn, we exited off the Autobahn and turned to enter the Army post, Wharton Barracks, where the battalion had assigned our Company. There were Signal Corps, Combat Engineers, and Military Police assigned to the post.

The small installation had three-story barracks that lined the main road running through the post and a paved parade field and parking area in the center. There were the normal post facilities, a small post exchange (department store), gas station, snack bar, commissary (grocery store), gym, and a youth center for the children of servicemen and servicewomen. The post had an enlisted club for E4 and below, NCO Club for E5 to E9, and an Officer club. A small medical clinic and dental clinic served the post, but I needed to travel to the Army Hospital at Stuttgart for any major medical or dental care. Right outside the post main gate was the military housing area, with many apartment buildings scattered on the hillside below the vineyards.

When the truck rolled to a stop, the driver yelled, "We are here." Vaydon and I grabbed our duffle bags and tossed them out the rear of the truck; then we jumped, landing hard on the ground, still on our feet. The First Sergeant greeted us and told us to come into his office. We picked up our bags and followed him. The First Sergeant was a white, six-foot career soldier in his mid-30s, and he had a slender build and spoke in a soft voice. He, too, had served in Vietnam.

The First Sergeant assigned me to 2nd platoon and Vaydon to 3rd platoon. He told us about the items that the military rationed, and how to use the issued ration cards. Ration cards prevented desirable merchandise: coffee, gasoline, liquor, and cigarettes to name a few, from being sold (in large quantities) on the German black market. He then briefed us on the Company mission and the makeup of the Company. The 2nd Battalion/4th Infantry Regiment, a bastard battalion comprising four rifle companies, with each Company responsible for guarding a Pershing Missile Battalion scattered throughout southern Germany. Each infantry Company operated as a separate entity.

Charlie Company had four light infantry platoons with each platoon made up of four ten-man squads. Each squad had two Sergeants as team leaders and a Staff Sergeant squad leader. Three squads were rifle squads, and the fourth squad was the weapons squad, with three M60 machine guns with assistant gunners and three grenade launchers. A 2nd Lieutenant platoon leader commanded the platoon, with a Sergeant First Class platoon sergeant and two drivers/radio operators.

Brigade had a requirement for the platoon leader and one NCO in the platoon to be Ranger qualified. The platoon had a jeep, two portable radios (AN/PRC-25) and two 2½ ton trucks with trailers for transportation assigned. Each squad leader had a portable radio that fit on the helmet, but it seldom worked.

The primary mission of the Company was guarding the Pershing Missiles and artillery personnel during missile deployments, and each platoon secured a Pershing Missile battery. Each missile had a nuclear warhead—one of the major deterrents in Europe. The Department of Army made a secret clearance and enrolled in the Surety Program, a requirement of every soldier assigned to the 56th Artillery Brigade. This program ensured that U.S. nuclear weapons were safe, secure, reliable, and under positive control, a concept commonly referred to as "surety."

The U.S. Army had control of the nuclear warheads because the German constitution didn't let its government have nuclear weapons. The missile system, a mobile system, which allowed deployment to clandestine sites during alerts or war was the most survivable nuclear weapon deployed in Europe. Battalion firing batteries deployed to unused tactical sites during periods of increased tension. A flatbed truck towed a modified flatbed trailer that held the missile with a hydraulic system that erected the missile for firing. The warhead wasn't attached to the missile during transport. After setting up in a tactical field position, the crew attached the warhead to the missile.

Once the missiles were fired, the mission of the infantry Company changed. We were to stay behind enemy lines and disrupt Russian movement of supplies and troops into Germany. Hence, the requirement of officers being Ranger qualified, with at least one Ranger-qualified NCO per platoon. With the dual missions, we seldom stopped training. If we were not guarding the missiles, we trained for small-unit tactics.

I joined the platoon, and the platoon Sergeant designated me as the third squad leader and assigned me to a private room in the barracks.

Figure 2-1 Neu Ulm Germany—a Battery of Pershing missiles. An infantry platoon guarded nine missiles. Photographer Jay Robinson.

The barracks had three floors with squad rooms for the soldiers to live and private rooms for the NCOs. The First Sergeant and Company Commander offices were on the first floor, and the supply room, arms room, mailroom, and platoon-leader offices were in the basement. The Company converted the attic to a classroom for training. I'd live in the barracks until quarters were available and then send for Paula and David.

The platoon sergeant, Staff Sergeant John Lee, was black and had a little darker complexion than me. He was around five years older, taller and heavier, with a round face that displayed a large, welcoming smile. Not long after I met John, he became my mentor. He was the best NCO I'd ever met, and he guided me in how to become a leader. Staff Sergeant Lee, a knowledgeable, articulate, and fair NCO, had a way in which he showed respect and authority when talking to Officers, NCOs, and soldiers. And he had patience, something I lacked. He received a promotion to Sergeant First Class several months after my arrival. Lieutenant Costello, short and chubby-looking but not overweight, and new to the Army, with little experience, was the platoon leader and a good officer. The other NCOs, team leaders, and squad leaders assigned to the platoon had combat experience in Vietnam, including the platoon sergeant. Few of the enlisted platoon members had served in Vietnam, and most were draftees.

Most of the NCOs in the Company were young and had been promoted quickly, while serving in Vietnam, to Sergeant and a few to Staff Sergeant. None of the platoon leaders had served in Vietnam, and they were fresh from Officer Candidate School (OCS) or Reserve Officers' Training Corps (ROTC). The leadership skills and knowledge of the Officers and NCOs were perhaps weaker than pre-Vietnam times because of the lack of experience and professional-education opportunities and maturity. With the draft ending, it was a volunteer Army, but many Sergeants had trained only as a squad leader in Vietnam and didn't know how to train soldiers. I fell into this category. Because I served in war as an infantry soldier doesn't mean I was mentally mature. Yes, I grew up fast and went to Vietnam as an 18-year-old and returned home feeling like a 35-year-old. The experiences of an 18- or 19-year-old might be the same as a much older person, but it doesn't mean his maturity level is the same. The rational part of a 19-year-old brain isn't fully developed until age 25. And I had received no professional education during my three and a half years in the Army.

RACE, DRUGS, AND ALCOHOL

I soon learned this would be the hardest three years of my military career. There were drug and alcohol abuse, racial intolerance, disobedience to authority, and, at times, outright unrest among the soldiers of the Company. I determined that there were five groups within the Company, and I named them: Rednecks, Black Power, Hispanic, Drug Users, and Noncommissioned Officers and Good Soldiers. The rednecks filled their ranks with white boys from every state, and they displayed racial hate and drank too much. Black power filled its ranks with black soldiers who felt oppressed by the "white man" and displayed their hate toward whites and anyone in authority. The Hispanics, I believe, united to protect each other from everyone else. The drug users were of every race and cared only about smoking pot or hash and mainlining heroin. The NCOs, regardless of race, banded together to keep some measure of discipline. This appeared an impossible task.

I often wondered why the NCOs and Good Soldiers and the Drug Abusers had little difficulty getting along with members of their groups, regardless of race. Maybe each group had a common cause that kept them united. The NCOs attempted to carry out the mission of the Company as professional soldiers. The good soldiers wanted to serve their time honorably. The drug abusers attempted to stay high so they didn't have to know what happened in the Company, so race didn't matter.

Racial unrest got so severe that the Army started Race Relations Training and required every soldier to attend once a year. Race Relations instructors came in pairs, a First Lieutenant and a Sergeant First Class, one black and the other white. The purpose of the training tried to highlight the racial injustice in America and allowed the soldiers to discuss their differences and prejudices. During training, the classroom could become very heated and, at times, volatile. I didn't have access to any statistical information gathered from the training, but I didn't see it helping in our Company in the short term. The training just seemed to piss everyone off even more.

The Army had been desegregated for years by the early 1970s. An executive order issued by President Truman on July 26, 1948, ended racial discrimination in the Armed Forces, and it ended segregation in the services, too. I believe disobedience to authority and drug use to be in direct correlation to the "peace" movement and universities. I believe many universities taught (either directly or indirectly) our youth that doing drugs and showing disobedience to authority were the norms. The soldiers in our Company using drugs had never served in war, so, in my eyes, the drug-use problem wasn't something that had been brought back from Vietnam. It wasn't happening only in Germany; it was happening in the units stationed in Korea and Vietnam, too.

The Army instituted a random drug test because the drug problem had started to become an epidemic. If a soldier tested positive on a drug test, he lost his security clearance and was transferred from the unit. Some soldiers deliberately tested positive so they could get out of the unit. I could walk into a squad room and find soldiers shooting up or smoking hash. The commander wanted an officer to catch the drug users in action and didn't recognize abuse when reported by an NCO. By the time I got an officer, the offending soldier had cleaned his room free of drugs or paraphernalia. I did reach the point where I hated to get up in the morning and go to work each day. This assignment depressed me!

I want to add that there were many good soldiers in the Company. Most were draftees and were committed to fulfilling their obligation honorably. They got up every morning, attended physical training, cleaned the barracks, made formations, moved out with the platoon for training, and performed as outstanding soldiers. These soldiers were from all races, didn't abuse drugs or alcohol, and didn't join in the racial hatred.

One morning after arriving at the barracks, the First Sergeant notified me that a soldier in my squad had died in his sleep. He drowned in his own vomit from drinking too much. The eight other soldiers in the room claimed they didn't hear the soldier puking or drowning, so the 17-year-old soldier didn't receive life-saving aid. I spent the morning packing his belongings to return to his parents' home and turned in his military equipment, along with his puke-soaked sheets, to the supply sergeant. The Company Commander prepared the death notification to his parents. His death marked a sad day. I didn't think I'd see another dead soldier again.

THE FIRST MONTHS

I learned that our mission was to pull security on the missile site, go to the field when the missile batteries trained, and go to the field to train for our secondary infantry mission. We were away more than we were at home with our families. When we went to the missile site, we pulled guard for a month and then rotated off the site back to the Company for three months. When on the site, we worked 24 hours on and 24 hours off but remained on the site, with one exception: we came home every 7 days for 12 hours. The soldiers had guard-tower duty with four hours on and four hours off each day. I believe there were eight towers. The platoon stayed in the barracks onsite, where we slept, played games, played poker, read, and ate. The NCOs were Sergeant of the Guard (SOG), and they checked on their squad members pulling guard in the towers and took patrols outside the fenced compound. We carried M16 rifles with ammunition while on guard duty. It was hard for our spouses and children because of our mission and training schedule. They were in a foreign country, and we were leaving them at home and alone; the isolation proved difficult for them.

The Pershing missile site had many layers of security—fenced areas inside fenced areas within the compound. We didn't have interaction with the artillery soldiers manning the Pershing missiles; they were in the innermost fenced area. If anyone breached the outside fence, we had a protocol in place to stop them, and that was to use deadly force.

We trained for our infantry mission at a training area with steep hills and heavily wooded forest a short distance from the post. When not onsite, we went to the field for three or four days a week to train for our infantry mission. We trained on small-unit tactics, setting up a perimeter, digging foxholes for defensive positions, fields of fire, patrolling techniques, and fire-and-maneuver to advance on enemy positions. We seldom used sleeping bags, tents, or any other shelter. We trained outside in the winter and inside during the summer months. Germany had freezing wet weather during the winter months. The constant exposure to the weather, hot or cold, got old quick.

During the summer months, the platoon had indoor formal classroom training and practiced drill and ceremony in the center courtyard in front of the barracks. We spent many hours in the motor pool making sure the vehicles and trailers were ready to move out at a moment's notice. Each platoon did infantry training during the summer, but it didn't happen as often as in the winter months. At times, it appeared we were training on how to be miserable while enduring harsh weather.

There were three formations daily—morning, noon, and evening—for accountability and to give out information to the Company. The Company Commander gave, sometimes, a three-day weekend training holiday, and every Thursday afternoon, we had organized sports. I played fast-pitch softball, basketball, and football on the Company team. We had physical training every Monday, Wednesday, and Friday. I ran on most evenings, setting a goal to run four miles in under 32 minutes. We ran in fatigue uniforms and combat boots during physical training, and I did the same when I ran in the evenings. We took our Army Physical Fitness Test (APFT) wearing a fatigue uniform and combat boots. I lost the weight gained at Fort Benning, weighing in at 160 pounds, and firm again from the exercise and workouts.

After three months with the Company, the First Sergeant called me to his office. This is normally not a good thing. I entered his office, we exchanged "Hellos," and he informed me that the Red Cross wanted to see me. My first thought hit hard—*My Dad has died, as he wasn't healthy when I left for Germany.* I walked across the courtyard toward the Red Cross office with my mind spinning, trying to determine what terrible news they would tell me. I opened the front door to the office and walked into a room with three wooden desks and a female Red Cross worker sitting in a wooden office chair behind each desk. I approached the desk on the right because she made eye contact as I entered the office.

A middle-aged woman with brown hair streaked with gray, plain, black-framed glasses, and a stern glare asked, "What can I do for you, Sergeant?"

"I'm Sergeant Haynie with Charlie Company, and my First Sergeant said you needed to see me," I responded.

She looked at papers on her desk and stated, in a matter-of-fact tone, "Your wife, Paula, wants a divorce."

I looked at her in disbelief and murmured, "OK." I turned around and exited the office. On my walk to the barracks, my mind raced again. I knew things were not perfect in the marriage, but this caught me by surprise.

Once back at the Company, I requested through my platoon sergeant to see the First Sergeant. I asked if I could get a two-week leave to fly back to the States and see my wife and child and try to fix the problem, and the First Sergeant agreed. Before leaving, I was fortunate to get a fellow soldier to hold his apartment until I got back from my leave. I told him I would call as soon as possible if I wanted the apartment. I flew from Frankfurt to Columbus, Georgia, a couple days later.

Shortly after arriving home, I called and told the soldier I wanted the apartment and gave him my arrival date. Within two weeks, Paula and David flew back to Germany with me. He picked us up at the Frankfurt airport, and we moved into the apartment several days later. I don't remember what the rent was, but I know we paid in German currency, the *mark*.

The apartment was small—maybe 800 square feet—sparsely furnished, and the appliances were smaller, too. This was how Germans lived. The apartment was fine for the three of us until quarters became available, and it was a short drive to work at Wharton Barracks. Within two months, the value of the dollar compared to the *mark* dropped by

50 percent, but that rate lasted only several weeks. Our rent could've doubled. Fortunately, within several weeks, military housing became available, and we moved before we felt the full impact of the rent increase. I never considered the currency conversion a problem.

We moved into military quarters, a third-floor apartment, with a large living/dining room combination and eat-in kitchen, two bedrooms, and one bath. The apartment had a total of 1200 square feet, and the Army provided the furniture. We kept the washer and dryer in the basement laundry room. I gave up my housing allowance and food allowance for payment, around $180 a month.

I don't think our marriage ever recovered after I'd learned at the Red Cross that Paula wanted a divorce, but we tried. Not long after we set up the house, Paula became pregnant with John William, soon to be my second son.

Another NCO, from Maine, by the name of Jeff Weatherbee, and I, became friends. The First Sergeant assigned Jeff to First platoon. Jeff was an inch taller than me and barrel-chested. He appeared to have some extra weight, but he was not overweight. He had light-brown hair and was a good-humored and fun person. From Maine, he had the Eastern New England accent, and it was entertaining to hear him talk and tell his stories.

Vaydon and his wife, Lynda, Jeff and his wife, Gloria, and Paula and I got together most weekends sharing dinner, talking, or playing cards. For the guys, most of our conversations centered on work and what our next assignment might be after our tour in Germany, and the wives talked of the isolation, their husbands being gone so much, and how they could support each other during our absence. Some Saturday nights we got babysitters and went to the NCO club to have dinner, drink, and listen to the band and dance, a good break from work. I still drank on weekends, but I'd stopped smoking grass before I arrived in Germany.

A LONG SUMMER

It was via the *Stars and Stripes* weekly newspaper, the U.S. military's independent news source, and Armed Forces Network (AFN) television

33

that we learned Jane Fonda had gone to Hanoi to encourage them, our enemy, in July 1972. She helped give North Vietnam and its army the will to continue fighting against her own countrymen. I either read an article or saw a video of Jane Fonda saying, "POWs should be tried, convicted, and executed" while she was in Hanoi. And there was the photo of her sitting, with a large smile on her face, at the anti-aircraft gun as though she was shooting down our military aircraft. She called returning POWs "hypocrites and liars" and said that the North Vietnamese never tortured them. I believe this speaks of her character and traitorous actions. Her visit caused much debate in the platoon, but I don't believe one combat veteran supported her. I know that most of us hated her for going to North Vietnam. I did. Many of us vowed to never watch a movie that she acted in or support her career in any way. I have honored that vow.

Fonda going to Hanoi brought back memories of her Free The Army (FTA) group, 1970 through 1971, that toured military bases in the States and abroad. It was an anti-Vietnam War road show designed as a response to Bob Hope's USO tour. Wow, Miss Fonda thinks Bob Hope supporting the U.S. troops wasn't a good thing to do! Fonda and Donald Sutherland, with other entertainers, started the show by making fun of the Army and its commitment to fight communism that was ordered by the President of the United States. Filmmakers even made a documentary that showed the tour at theaters. I often thought "Hanoi Jane" and her colleagues needed to be with my platoon in Vietnam and experience communism up close. How can educated people be so naïve? I don't mean about supporting or not supporting the war but about communism as a way of life; she appeared to support it.

On one pleasant summer evening, I was at the NCO club having a steak dinner and drinks, and listening to a band with many other NCOs and their wives and girlfriends. I don't recall who was with me this specific evening. I noticed that the noise in the club was decreasing, and I heard angry voices coming from outside of the club. All hell broke loose. Black soldiers from our Company and other units on Wharton Barracks had incited a riot. Soldiers were throwing rocks and bottles at the club and yelling profanities and the slogan "Black Power" at the NCOs and wives. The club manager ran to the front door and locked it. Most NCOs stood together—black, white, Hispanic—ready to stop anyone from entering the front door.

I'd never experienced soldiers behaving like this. In time, they moved on to another part of the post. I later learned the rioting soldiers confronted the military police (MP) station and barracks with the same anger. The MPs barricaded their building so no one could enter. Within several hours, a reinforced MP unit arrived from Frankfurt to break up the riot. I learned later that riots had broken out on the Pershing missile post, Artillery Kaserne, around five miles from our post, but were contained within several hours. The next morning, I heard a rumor that soldiers hoisted the Black Power flag on the post flagpole on Artillery Kaserne.

We made it back to our quarters without incident. To this day, I don't know what sparked the outrage from the rioting soldiers, but I was glad it ended. Monday morning was another training day, no different from any other. I didn't know if any of my squad or platoon members had taken part in the riot. None of my platoon or Company soldiers faced charges for what happened that night.

Drugs and racial intolerance weren't the only problems, nor was the possibility of Russia invading Germany. We had to stay vigilant watching for terrorists. The Baader-Meinhof Gang was a West German far-left militant group and considered a part of the Red Army Faction that the East German state security supported. The German government and the U.S. Army suspected them of bombings, assassinations, and bank robberies, to name a few of their criminal activities; they were dangerous people. There were many times during my tour that the Company and our families went on alert because of suspected terrorist activity by the Baader-Meinhof Gang.

At the Summer Olympics in Munich, September 1972, 11 Israeli Olympic team members were taken hostage and later killed. The Palestinian terrorist group Black September was responsible for the attack on the Israeli Olympic team members. The terrorists demanded that Israel release more than 200 prisoners from their jails and that Germany release the founders of the Red Army Faction, Baader and Meinhof, from German prisons. Munich was a 190-mile drive south of Heilbronn. Our unit wasn't placed on alert, but we expected the worst while following the news reports. We watched the events unfold on German and Armed Forces Network television, hoping that the situation wouldn't escalate and cause the Company to move to the missile tactical sites. The standoff lasted less than 24 hours before German police officers killed five of the eight terrorists and captured the other three, ending the crisis.

LEADERSHIP TRAINING

I believed my leadership skills effective as a squad leader but wanted formal leadership training. Not because I thought of myself of being a poor leader, but I was growing aware that I needed formal training in counseling soldiers, completing needed paperwork at squad and platoon level, and garrison duties: drill and ceremonies, and conducting and preparing for inspections and parades, to name a few. I remained proficient in my squad and platoon tactical and technical skills, and my squad members never questioned my abilities in the field.

NCOs considered the four-week course at the 7th Army NCO Academy the premier NCO Academy in the Army, the same one Staff Sergeant Yulee had recommended. Most Army posts had an NCO Academy, but the rumor in the Army spread that no other academy matched the 7th Army NCO Academy. My luck and persistence paid off. A slot became available, and the First Sergeant scheduled me to attend. The Academy was 210 miles from Heilbronn, a three-and-a-half-hour drive south to Bad Tolz, near the Austrian border.

I reported on a Sunday afternoon, and the Academy cadre assigned me to a room with another Sergeant. The Academy furnished each room with two bunks, wall lockers, footlockers, and desks; one side of the room mirrored the other. We had to keep our room spotless with our clothing and personal articles in a specific location and order, similar to basic training. All students took turns using paste wax and a buffer to polish the Academy floor surfaces to a bright shine. We never walked on the center of the hallway, walking only along the left and right sides, as was the tradition. We learned leadership, drill and ceremony, land navigation, counseling with associated record-keeping, and other skills that require proficiency in leaders. The academy students conducted physical training daily, and we had to pass the APFT before graduation. The APFT consisted of the inverted crawl, run, dodge, and jump, horizontal ladder, bent knee sit-up, and a two-mile run. Female soldiers took a different physical training test. How many repetitions and how fast you had to run the two miles depended on your age; the requirement decreased as I got older. There were no female soldiers at the Academy.

Monday morning, we formed for the first formation of the day and class. An academy cadre NCO stood at attention in front of the formation and bellowed, "Sergeant Haynie, front and center!" I left my position and ran to the front of the formation, stopped, and stood at attention facing the NCO. I had no idea why he'd called me to the front of the formation. As I stood in front of the NCO, my brain raced, trying to remember if I messed up somehow! The NCO ordered, "You are now the class commander. Move the class to the mess hall for chow." Then he saluted, and I returned the salute. Executing an about-face, he walked away, leaving the formation. I thought, *Oh, shit! I have never marched a unit in my short military career.*

To face the class, I executed an about-face. In a shaky voice, I gave the command, "Right" and, with a short pause, "Face" and executed the command with the class as they faced to the right. I then gave the command "Forward" and, with a short pause, "March," and the class stepped off with their left foot and marched forward. Within minutes, I had the class marching in many directions, blocking the morning traffic and taking ten minutes to go the 200 meters to the mess hall. For example, I gave commands to turn left when I should've commanded them to turn right. In good time, the four NCOs up front leading each squad ignored my commands and marched the class the last 50 feet to the mess hall. What an embarrassment! Once they halted, I ordered the class to enter the mess hall in single file, and, as they passed by, several classmates gave me words of encouragement. I was nervous, and this was the first time I'd ever marched soldiers. I stayed up late many nights learning drill and ceremony. My leadership position lasted a week, and then another NCO got his turn.

I studied hard and learned as much as I could—particularly, the necessary garrison skills. My tactical and technical skills were still sharp, and I helped NCOs who didn't have infantry experience with squad and platoon tactics, weapons, and map reading, and many NCOs helped me with my garrison skills. It took teamwork to graduate. After graduation, I reported back to Charlie Company and its many problems. But I believed I'd improved my leadership skills and was now a better NCO.

During my time at the NCO Academy, I decided to make the Army a career and be a career soldier and leader. One requirement we had was to memorize the Creed of the NCO. At first, I thought of the assignment as a waste of time and a chore, but the more I read it and committed the Creed to memory, the more I understood what it meant to be a professional Noncommissioned Officer. It no longer became an assignment—or just words—but something to guide and remind me throughout my Army career. This is the Creed of the Noncommissioned Officer and the standard I tried to hold myself to:

NCO CREED

No one is more professional than I. I am a noncommissioned officer, a leader of Soldiers. As a noncommissioned officer, I realize that I am a member of a time-honored Corps, which is known as "The Backbone of the Army." I am proud of the Corps of noncommissioned officers and will at all times conduct myself so as to bring credit upon the Corps, the military service, and my country regardless of the situation in which I find myself. I will not use my grade or position to attain pleasure, profit, or personal safety.

Competence is my watchword. My two basic responsibilities will always be uppermost in my mind—accomplishment of my mission and the welfare of my Soldiers. I will strive to remain technically and tactically proficient. I am aware of my role as a noncommissioned officer. I will fulfill my responsibilities inherent in that role. All Soldiers are entitled to outstanding leadership; I will provide that leadership. I know my Soldiers and I will always place their needs above my own. I will communicate consistently with my Soldiers and never leave them uninformed. I will be fair and impartial when recommending both rewards and punishment.

Officers of my unit will have maximum time to accomplish their duties; they will not have to accomplish mine. I will earn their respect and confidence as well as that of my Soldiers. I will be loyal to those with whom I serve; seniors, peers, and subordinates alike. I will exercise initiative by taking appropriate action in the absence of orders. I will not compromise my integrity or my moral courage. I will not forget, nor will I allow my comrades to forget, that we are professionals, noncommissioned officers, leaders!

A TRAIN RIDE

At the end of the summer of 1972, I asked my mother-in-law, Nell, to ship my Camaro to Germany. The Army would pay to have it shipped. Nell drove the car to the port at Charleston, South Carolina, and had it shipped to Bremerhaven, Germany, the main port in northern Germany. The Army transportation office in Bremerhaven notified me when my car arrived, 30 days after it had shipped from Charleston. Sergeant First Class Lee gave me two days off to make the trip to Bremerhaven to pick up my car and drive back to Heilbronn.

I purchased a one-way train ticket to Bremerhaven and went to the Heilbronn train station. It was a small station, and I had no problem catching the train out of Heilbronn, but I needed to switch trains in

Frankfurt. Once the train pulled into Frankfurt, I stepped off the train steps, and the station overwhelmed me. There were hundreds of tracks and boarding areas for trains arriving and departing to many cities and thousands of passengers coming and going. All I saw was mass chaos! I walked along one track, thinking it the correct direction, and stopped where passengers boarded the train from a platform. But I was unsure that I had the correct train. As passengers walked past me, I tried to ask for help, but no one admitted to speaking English, and I didn't know enough German. They walked on by, ignoring my request for help.

Standing on the platform, confused, I looked into a window of the passenger car in front of me and saw an elderly woman, around 75 years old. She was wearing a fox stole around her neck, a small hat, tilted on her head, and a matching blue jacket and skirt. She stood and walked to the exit door of the train. Tightly gripping the railing to help keep her balance, with her head held high and body erect, she stepped down the steps onto the platform and then approached me.

With a heavy German accent, but in near-perfect English, she asked, "Can I help you, young man?"

Relief washed over my body, and, smiling, I replied, "Yes, ma'am. I am going to Bremerhaven, but I'm not sure which train is mine. Can you help me?"

With a smile, she said, "You're at the correct train. Come sit with me."

While helping the elderly lady up the steps, I said "Thank you" many times. We walked along the narrow aisle of the passenger car, with me following to the seat she'd occupied before getting off the train to help. The two of us sat and talked during the long trip to Bremerhaven. She told of the years during World War II and how much the German people appreciated the Americans. Most of her stories about the War concerned the hardships of the Allied bombings, rationing of food and other comfort items, and the loss of life on all sides, including her husband. I soon learned the older people in Germany had a greater appreciation for the American presence in Germany than the younger generation did.

There were no other problems in getting to the port or in picking up the Camaro for the seven-hour drive to Heilbronn. The yellow Camaro got many stares speeding along the Autobahn, and, with a smile, I was thinking, *Wow! I'm doing 100 miles an hour without straining.* I'd missed the Camaro, and now I no longer had to drive the old beat-up Volkswagen I'd purchased when first arriving in Germany; I sold it to another NCO. Soldiers bought these older cars when arriving in Germany and resold them when leaving, a continuous buying-and-selling cycle for the car.

The platoon continued to go to the missile site one month out of every three and then to the local training area several days a week. The training schedule put a strain on family life. When in garrison, not on the missile site, on occasion, we had Adventure Training. This training was to build teamwork and morale and was not necessarily mission driven.

CLIMBING A MOUNTAIN

In late fall of 1972, the Company trained for mountain climbing. Zugspitze was the mountain to conquer. The Zugspitze peaks at 9,718 feet high and is the highest mountain in Germany. It lies south of the town of Garmisch-Partenkirchen, near the Austrian border. Our training consisted of more physical training and leg-strengthening exercises. We were not scaling the cliffs but walking up a known trail from the base of the mountain to the top. The route the Company took didn't require technical mountain-climbing skills.

The Company ascended the mountain by platoons in the early morning, with heavy, wet snowflakes and a freezing light wind blowing. Each soldier wore a fatigue uniform with long underwear under the uniform, leather gloves with wool inserts, standard-issue combat boots with wool socks, and a field jacket with a liner for the climb. While walking along the rocky, wet, frozen, and barren trail, I thought of the mountains I'd climbed in Vietnam. The only similarities were being wet and tired. In Vietnam, the trail ran through dense jungle vegetation, and sometimes we had to cut our way through while looking for the enemy and crossing swift-flowing streams that could carry a man downstream. I snapped back to reality as the German mountain troops, the *Bundeswehr*, descended the mountain and we passed each German soldier one-by-one on the way to the top. I'm sure the expression I saw on the soldiers' faces was a look of disbelief that the dumb Americans were continuing up the mountain.

The goal was to reach the mountaintop, where there was a restaurant, and eat a dinner meal before dark. The climb was difficult following the narrow, wet trail and navigating the many bends and turns leading to the top. In no time, my legs ached, and my breathing became labored. Everyone in the platoon helped each other and arrived at the restaurant with enough daylight to enjoy the stunning view of the mountains and valleys—well worth the climb. After a good German meal—*Weiner Schnitzel*, which is veal thinned by pounding with a meat tenderizer and fried—the platoons loaded onto the cable cars for the ride back to the base of the mountain, where we'd left the trucks parked. The view was spectacular, but riding on the cable car scared me more than climbing the mountain.

Figure 2–2 Two squads of the second platoon at the top of the Zugspitze, 1972. Me squatting in the second row, first on your left. Photographer unknown.

The Christmas season came and went. We got plenty of time off the last two weeks of December. I had time to spend with Paula and David for David's second Christmas. Being older, he had a better understanding about Santa and presents this year. We had fun.

I had CQ New Year's Eve. The arms room issued the CQ a 45-caliber pistol, with one magazine of ammunition loaded into the pistol, ready for any hostile troop behavior, including drug- or alcohol-induced violence or racially motivated assaults. Fortunately, I never had to pull the pistol to defend myself or another soldier. I stayed awake and made sure there were no fires, fights, or other disruptions in the barracks. While on CQ, I would receive any emergency-deployment notifications, so I had an alert roster to call the officers and NCOs.

Figure 2–3 Me on top of the Zugspitze, 1972. Photographer unknown.

One evening, a black soldier, coaxed by his peers, attacked the CQ and tried to wrestle the pistol away. The CQ and Assistant CQ wrestled him to the ground and held him until the Military Police (MP) arrived. The MPs arrested him, and he received a court-martial and a two-year prison sentence. Receiving a sentence of more than three years would have put him in the military prison in Leavenworth, Kansas. I transported him to the Military Corrections Facility in Mannheim, Germany. Mannheim is a city in southwest Germany between Heilbronn and Frankfurt, on the Rhine and Neckar rivers. He gave me a sad look when I turned him over to the prison. I felt sorry for him, a good soldier who got mixed up with the wrong people and the opposite of the soldier Mike Dankert and I had taken to the Long Binh Jail (LBJ) in Vietnam.

On Monday, January 15, 1973, the Company was preparing to go to the local training area for three days. As usual, squad leaders in each platoon readied their squads by drawing weapons and having each soldier get their equipment ready. The platoons moved to the front of the barracks for formation. I don't remember the exact number of black soldiers, maybe 15, refused to go to the field that day. These soldiers had proclaimed this day, Martin Luther King Jr.'s birthday, a holiday, and they wouldn't work this day. The platoons got on their assigned trucks and drove out the front gate without the 15 soldiers. To the best of my memory, these 15 soldiers received no punishment. Morale in the Company sank lower.

January 1973—I'm 22 years old, married, with one child, and still in Germany after completing one year. I have two more years left on this assignment.

CHAPTER 3

WAYNE ARRIVES

*"The truth of the matter is that you always know the right thing to do.
The hard part is doing it."*

—GENERAL NORMAN SCHWARZKOPF

Wayne had contacted me and told me he had orders for Germany. I talked with the First Sergeant to see if he could help me in getting Wayne assigned to the Company. The First Sergeant called his contacts and made it happen. Wayne knew he was reporting to Charlie Company before he arrived.

Not long after January 15, 1973, Wayne flew into Frankfurt, one year after me. I picked him up at the airport and drove back to my quarters. Wayne stayed with us until he could find a place to live. The housing list had soldiers waiting a year until quarters were available. Wayne found a small farmhouse to rent on an older German couple's farm. The rental house had the barn attached to the back of the house, and sometimes the odor became strong. Otherwise, Wayne and his family had a great home to live in. Wayne sent for Dee and his daughter, Traci, as soon as he signed the lease. The nice, older German couple treated Wayne and Dee as their adopted children.

Having Wayne and Dee joining us in Germany made the tour tolerable, and they fit in well with the Weatherbees and Jacobs. Now there were four couples having dinner, picnics, talking, playing cards, and helping each other. The First Sergeant assigned Wayne to a different platoon, so sometimes we didn't see each other for a while because of the scheduling for missile-site duty and field training. During my time with Wayne, Vaydon, and Jeff, I learned valuable lessons from each on how to be a better NCO.

The month after Wayne arrived, February 1973, the Army promoted me to Staff Sergeant (E6). I now had four years and seven months in the Army. Finally, the Army lifted the freeze on promotions. I lost more than a year of time in which I could've been a Staff Sergeant, but I was proud of the promotion and happy to get paid for the position I had been working.

The Company still had the racial and drug problems it had when I'd arrived a year earlier. There were many Article 15s given, but the problems continued. An Article 15 was non-judicial punishment in the Uniform Code of Military Justice. It permitted local commanders to administratively discipline troops without a court-martial. The NCOs and officers did the best they could to keep order and train for our missions. At one point, the Battalion Commander ordered the Company Commander to stop giving Article 15s, because he gave so many. I don't believe stopping helped, either.

The Battalion Commander relieved—fired—the Company Commander and First Sergeant in late 1973, for the drug and racial problems, and we received replacements for both. The platoon received a new platoon leader, Sergeant First Class Bruce Straussfogel, a white, short, Special Forces NCO, during this transition. There wasn't a Lieutenant available, so the Company Commander assigned Sergeant First Class Straussfogel. He proved to be a good, fair leader and was later assigned as the Company First Sergeant. With the leadership of Sergeant First Class Straussfogel and Sergeant First Class Lee, I saw improvement within the platoon. Both were technically and tactically proficient.

In the summer of 1973, the Command scheduled another adventure-training exercise for the Company. We would learn to float downstream on the river using inflatable rubber rafts. Each raft held ten men, equipped with oars. The training prepared us for the task of paddling downstream on the Neckar River. The Neckar is a 228-mile-long river in Germany that flows primarily through the southwestern state of Baden-Württemberg. I don't recall how far or what the real goal might have been. I remembered a planned five-day trip and stopping at night at a predetermined location to eat dinner and sleep. We'd get up the next morning, have breakfast, and head along the river.

The instructors, I believe a First Lieutenant and Staff Sergeant who were Ranger qualified, taught us the best methods of getting into the boat, storing gear, and rowing. They thought it necessary to teach us how to react when a boat capsized, the worst part of the training. The squad would move to one side of the raft and make it flip over, with the bottom of the raft skyward. Once the flipped raft dumped us into the river, I did a headcount of the squad, and then we swam to one side and flipped the boat back over, which is much harder than it sounds.

I had one soldier who couldn't swim well and refused to get on the raft. I convinced him to take part by telling him I'd be there alongside him during the entire training session. Fortunately, he didn't know I wasn't a strong swimmer. When we capsized the raft, the squad went overboard into the slow-moving, cold, murky water, but the soldier who couldn't swim drifted under the raft. I swam under the raft, grabbed him, and pulled him out so he could hang onto the raft with the rest of the squad. He threw his arms around me, with his body thrashing in the water; I thought he'd take me under the water with him. He calmed as I talked to him, and he held onto the raft with a death grip.

We got it uprighted on the water and climbed back onboard. He refused to do any more raft training after getting stuck under the raft.

The Company Commander wanted to give him an Article 15, but I talked him out of it. A good soldier afraid of water didn't deserve punishment. After training hard for the adventure training, the Company schedule had my platoon guarding the missile site during the time of the river raft trip. We didn't go rafting. I had one happy squad member!

DEPLOY THE NUKES FOR WAR

On October 6, 1973, Egypt and Syria attacked Israel's forces in the Sinai Peninsula and the Golan Heights. The Soviets then resupplied Egypt and Syria with weapons. Not wanting to see Israel defeated, America supplied weapons by plane to Israel. The Company Commander said the rumor was the Russians had a division in the air circling the Mideast, and we were putting the 82nd on alert and in the air. The Company Commander issued orders to draw weapons and the basic load of ammunition from the arms room, and we were to join the Pershing missile Battalion when they deployed with warheads.

He gave the married personnel time to go to our quarters and make sure our families had their evacuation documentation and rations, and understood where they were to go for evacuation. I told the squad to get their gear ready and that I'd be back to give a briefing on our mission. Paula, around seven months pregnant with John, prepared for the evacuation before I arrived.

As I drove into the housing area, there was a jeep manned by two MPs driving through the neighborhood with a loudspeaker blaring instructions for all dependents to prepare for evacuation. I parked and went upstairs to our apartment, and Paula and I went through the checklist and made sure we had the required documents and other necessities: c-rations, water, and extra clothes. We never thought we would use this checklist. There were some older NCO wives who had experience, and they volunteered to make sure Paula and David got to where they needed to be, but Paula said she would check on Dee first. Wayne was on the missile site. I drove Paula and David to Wayne's quarters; we said our goodbyes, and I left for the Company. On the five-minute drive back to the barracks, it hit me that this alert meant we might go to war.

When I got back to the barracks, I called the squad together to brief them on our mission, and everyone appeared tense. I wanted someone with combat experience to carry the M60 machine gun, so during the briefing, I said to Sergeant Rupp, a team leader, "M60, you are on the Sergeant Rupp." The room broke out in laughter, and within seconds I realized what I'd said to Sergeant Rupp. I laughed along with the squad and corrected myself: "Sergeant Rupp, you are on the M60." I believe this statement eased the tension, and I was fine with that.

We loaded into our trucks by platoons, and the Company headed to the staging area, where the Pershing missiles would be. We drove deep into a wooded area, with plenty of cover and concealment. When we arrived, the platoon unloaded and moved out to secure the perimeter around the battery we supported, which had nine armed nuclear warheads. We knew this might be for real. The platoon remained for several days before we were ordered to return to Wharton Barracks. The crisis had ended, and we were back performing our daily training schedule.

Within ten days, the threat died down, and Egypt and Syria sought peace with Israel. This war brought the United States closer to a nuclear confrontation with the Soviet Union more than at any point since the Cuban missile crisis. As a result, the Arab oil producers established an embargo of oil shipments to the United States, causing fuel shortages. The embargo made us cut back on training.

In early winter each year, we went to Grafenwöhr or Hohenfels training area for a graded Field Training Exercise (FTX). These lasted for two weeks. We would drive by truck and stay in a barracks during the weekend but were in the field on weekdays. The gas shortage prevented this training exercise in 1973, and we didn't go. The evaluators graded us as a squad, a platoon, and Company for our support mission, security of the Pershing Missiles. We lived in foxholes without shelter or sleeping bags. I had never been this cold before these training exercises. I wanted to quit, but I acted as an NCO should and braved the weather.

Packing up at the end of these exercises and heading back to Heilbronn made my day. Our squad, platoon, and Company always did well on their evaluations. I remember these training locations being wet, muddy, and freezing, and the sky always overcast and dark.

We had infantry FTX graded exercises at our local training area. Battalion staff officers and NCOs were the evaluators. The evaluation lasted for three days. They graded small-unit tactics, land navigation, and first-aid skills, to name a few. During the Battalion graded squad exercises each year, my squad performed well: first place in 1972 and second place in 1973 and 1974.

DRIVING TO STUTTGART

On December 3, 1973, Paula woke me up and said she had started labor. I called Wayne and told him we were going to the hospital and would leave David with him. I gathered the overnight bag and loaded Paula, David, and the bag into the Camaro on a cold winter morning. I dropped David off with Dee, as we had arranged for earlier.

We sped along the Autobahn for the 40-minute drive to the military hospital in Stuttgart. With 15 minutes remaining on the trip, my windshield fogged up, so I couldn't see, and the heater quit working. I rolled down the driver's-side window so I could see out the window and tried to defog the windshield. With my head hanging out the open window and the wet freezing air hitting me in the face, I watched the center line and continued to drive.

Once we arrived at the hospital, I unloaded Paula and the overnight bag and took her into the emergency room. The orderly at the desk admitted her, and another orderly took her upstairs. I was told to wait in the fathers waiting room. Within hours, the nurse told me I had a healthy son, John William.

Wayne picked me up at the hospital and took me to get my car. The thermostat gasket needed replacing in the car, and a German automobile shop mechanic installed a new one by tracing and cutting out a gasket from a manila folder. German automobile dealers or shops didn't carry

American car parts. I picked Paula and John up two days later and brought them home. When John arrived on December 3, 1973, I called my parents to let them know and told my dad I had named John after him. My dad, a long-time alcoholic, quit drinking that day.

Weeks after replacing the gasket, the engine sounded rough. One soldier in the squad said he repaired cars before coming into the Army and that he'd look at my car. After a quick analysis, he told me the carburetor needed replacing or rebuilding. Not able to find or order the part needed, I asked my dad to send a carburetor-rebuild kit. I received it in ten days and asked the soldier to meet me at the motor pool to install the rebuild kit. With the hood open and the carburetor removed, he asked me to turn the key and press the gas pedal. When I did as asked, the engine erupted in flames. He immediately grabbed the fire extinguisher and put out the fire—but not fast enough. The fire singed several spark-plug cables, and a large spot on the hood of the car burned, melting the paint. The mechanic finished installing the rebuild kit, and the car ran fine. I never used a backyard mechanic again.

FRENCH COMMANDO SCHOOL

In the spring of 1974, the Company Commander asked for volunteers to attend the French Commando School in Breisach, Germany, a short distance from the Rhine River and the Black Forest, a mountainous region in southwest Germany, bordering France. The Rhine River separated the two countries. The French Commando Course was similar, in some of the physical requirements, to the Army Ranger course, but much easier. Ranger school lasted nine weeks. They stayed out in the field most of the time and went without food and sleep. We called the French Commando Course a "mini-Ranger Course," but we had hot meals, and, most nights, we slept in a bunk. The Rangers seldom had either during their course. This course taught small-unit tactics, patrolling, and leadership, but the biggest focus of the course was on teamwork. There were many obstacle courses, and we carried a pack with an M1 rifle everywhere we went.

I volunteered, and so did Wayne. I saw an opportunity to get away from the Company for three weeks. I still hated getting up and going to work every day. In no time, we had a full platoon of volunteers. It appeared I wasn't the only one who wanted to get away from the Company.

The Company Commander gave the platoon 30 days to prepare for the course and exempted us from any other duties. He wanted all the members of the platoon to graduate—no quitters. The rumor spread that no American platoon had made it through the course without soldiers quitting. I helped the platoon train and prepare for the course. We did a daily run up and down the vineyards, sometimes twice a day, and exercise to build upper-body strength. The platoon practiced rappelling from cliffs in the training area outside post. Staff Sergeant Sabin, a Ranger, trained us in the rappelling and mountain-climbing techniques needed for the course. We conducted land-navigation training and first-aid training, with teamwork the most important aspect. Graded course work required the squad members to complete each exercise together; the squad didn't finish with a task or obstacle until the last man of the squad finished. This wasn't an individual course. The platoon understood the course to be physically and mentally challenging.

When the departure date for the course arrived, the Company Commander made Staff Sergeant Gene Malone the platoon sergeant for the platoon attending the course. He hadn't trained with the platoon. Gene, a black NCO, was tall, with a medium-but-muscular build, and had been a Drill Sergeant before coming to the Company. He still wore the Drill Sergeant face, but I thought it had little impact on the soldiers. I liked and respected Gene. Gene outranked me, having more time in grade. It disappointed me not being the Platoon Sergeant, but I remained excited about attending the training. The platoon loaded into two trucks pulling trailers with our gear and headed to the French compound in Breisach.

We drove more than 125 miles south for around three hours. Once we pulled into the French post and stopped, several French NCOs greeted us. We jumped off the rear of the trucks, and the instructors showed us to our barracks. We learned that they didn't speak English and none of us spoke French. Wayne and I remembered a little of the French we learned while living in France as youngsters. It didn't help. This course would be an "I show, and you do" course.

The barracks were like American barracks. There were double bunk beds, one stacked over the other, and wall lockers to store our gear away. Wayne chose the lower, and I got the upper. We put our gear away and went out front for formation. The Commandant talked to us in French with some English. I didn't understand what he said. Once the Commandant finished, he repeated three times, "Hip, Hip, Boys!" and, as instructed, we replied, "Hooray" each time. We didn't understand the purpose or what the Commandant's chant meant; we followed the instructions of our instructors.

The instructors guided us to the mess hall for dinner. We sat by squads at four large wooden tables with wooden chairs. The French cooks brought out the meal in large bowls and serving plates. Every meal they served was "family style." We used actual plates and flatware to eat our food. This was unusual for us because we were used to filling individual trays served by the helpers in our mess hall. We had to learn to share the food equally. Most meals were hot, filling, and good tasting. They consisted of a meat, chicken, pork or beef, two or three vegetables, and bread with butter or jam. At most meals, I found the meat under-cooked for my tastes, but, of course, I ate the meat, anyway. Breakfast appeared to lack the protein we normally ate. I remember having bread, jam, fruit, and hot chocolate or coffee served for breakfast. I still didn't drink coffee and found the hot chocolate delicious and superior in taste compared to the instant hot chocolate I drank in Vietnam or got in the Company mess hall. The breakfast meal hit the spot for me because I seldom ate a big breakfast. The next morning, the training began.

French instructors graded us on a variety of exercises requiring the squads to use teamwork to successfully complete assigned tasks. With packs and M1 rifles slung across our backs, we negotiated obstacle courses that forced us to use every member of our squad to complete each course. Most obstacles were high in the trees. We rappelled from towers, walls, and cliffs, some more than 100 feet high, and learned to scale walls just as high. The squad ran to an obstacle, and after all squad members had completed the obstacle, it was on to another. Our time didn't stop until the last squad member crossed the finished line.

One training day, the squad moved from the morning formation to the building across the parade field. One instructor stood in the middle of the road, with his hands on his hips, looking down the long stretch of road. Within minutes, a tank rumbled along the road toward the instructor. He didn't flinch or move until I thought the tank would run over him. With both hands, he grabbed the lip of the tank halfway up to the turret and held on, allowing the tank to drag him across the pavement. After 30 seconds, he let go, and the tank drove over him. Once the tank passed over him, he jumped up, and we applauded in amazement.

The instructor pointed at me and signaled for me to stand where he'd stood earlier. Another tank came rumbling toward me. This time, it appeared the tank was moving faster; it sounded louder and looked larger. The instructor stepped aside and pointed at the tank. I waited until the tank gun barrel loomed over me and then grabbed the lip with both hands and held on for my life, allowing my body to go underneath the tank and drag me. I closed my eyes, not wanting to see the bottom of the tank as it flattened me into the pavement. Allowing the tank to drag me for 30 seconds, I let go. The tank rumbled over me and continued along the road. I jumped up with a big smile—I'd lived through it! Wayne, assigned to my squad, moved to the starting point, next to go, and the tank took him for a ride. The squad went one after another, enjoying the fear and the ride.

After the last squad member finished, the instructor dropped into a pushup position at the edge of the road, facing the direction from which the tanks had appeared earlier. When the tank approached him, he reached with his right hand, holding the pushup position with his left hand on the ground, touched the track, and rolled out of the way as the tank drove past him as he hit the ground. He pointed at me and the ground where he'd assumed the pushup position. I dropped into the pushup position, waited for the tank, and emulated what the instructor had shown. I learned that the French instructors expected the NCOs to do the task first. I thought it made sense; I was to lead by example. Each squad member followed me, one after another, touching the track from a pushup position and then rolling out of the way of the moving tank. The squad members and I surmised after the training session that the purpose of the tank training was to overcome the fear of approaching armored vehicles. We all agreed that it helped.

The French were big on boxing, which surprised me. In a large building across the parade field stood a boxing ring, with gloves and training equipment. The French Commandant relayed to the platoon that he had a boxing champion in his detachment.

In broken English, he shouted, "Fight Lui in the ring de boxe?"

Without thinking, I said, "My brother, Wayne, will!"

Wayne gave me a dirty look, but he didn't refuse the fight. To Wayne's credit, he'd never trained as a boxer, but he could be mean as hell when needed.

The afternoon of the fight, the French cadre and our platoon gathered around the ring. I laced up Wayne's gloves and gave him boxing advice. I'm sure he dismissed my advice because he knew I didn't have a clue about boxing. The French fighter climbed through the ropes and danced around the ring. Hell, he wasn't much bigger than me, and Wayne had him by 15 pounds. He had a slim build and moved fast.

The Commandant, the referee, called Wayne and the French soldier into the center of the ring and gave them instructions in French. I was hoping Wayne understood. The fight would be three rounds. Before the fight started, I made bets that Wayne would win. When the bell rang, Wayne moved out of his corner with unswerving quick steps, approaching his opponent and threw blows at the French soldier's head and body. The fight didn't last one round. The referee called the fight within 60 seconds after Wayne beat the shit out the French boxer. I bet Wayne only got hit once—by luck. When Wayne walked back to his corner, I said, "Wasn't that easy?" He gave me another of those big-brother looks.

Now Wayne had a fight manager—me! During the dinner meal that evening, one of the squad leaders told me that Sergeant Jordan had boxed in Golden Glove tournaments and said he could beat Wayne in the ring with little effort. I took offense to that comment and scheduled a fight. The Commandant agreed to referee the fight. Jordan, a powerfully built black man, shorter than Wayne, had huge arms and chest. The Commandant scheduled the fight for three rounds, and I took wagers for this fight, too.

Both fighters got into the ring, and the bell rang. They moved into the center of the ring and exchanged punches; I saw this fight would be different. Near the end of the second round, Jordan hit Wayne hard with a right cross. I saw his eyes glaze, and then his knees buckled. He didn't fall, and the bell rang. Wayne stumbled into the corner, and I washed off his face with cold water, and he took drinks from the canteen. While he was in the corner, I gave him the best advice a manager, or little brother, could give: "Stay the hell away from him!" The bell rang, and he went back into the ring. Blows were exchanged, but neither boxer got hurt. The fight ended as a draw. After the fight, Wayne called me aside and said, "No more fights" while giving me that big-brother look.

During the week of the boxing matches, training continued. One day, the squad ran to an isolated training site around four miles from the post. Several French instructors and many caged chickens greeted us. The instructors showed how to kill, pluck, or skin a chicken and how to use sticks to make a fire to cook the chicken for a meal. The chicken we caught would be our dinner meal. We broke into teams of two; Wayne and I formed a team. The instructors let the chickens out of the cages, and they ran everywhere. Wayne and I chased one chicken, cornered her, and then Wayne grabbed her by the feet. I told Wayne to pluck the feathers or skin the chicken and clean it, and I'd build a fire and cook the chicken. I had to rub two sticks together to get a flame that ignited the fire. Once Wayne had killed and cleaned the chicken, I cooked it, and we had dinner. We were hungry by this time, so we had a tasty chicken meal.

At the end of the second week, the squad boarded a French helicopter for a graded exercise. We were to fly along the Rhine River at a
low altitude, and the squad would jump into the river one by one and
then swim to shore, where the French instructors were waiting for us.
It sounded simple enough. The pilot flew as low as possible and made
many quick movements on the sticks. I think he tried to make us sick. As
we flew low, following along the river, I thought of the many helicopter
combat assaults I'd flown on in Vietnam. The crew chief interrupted my
thoughts and indicated we were approaching the drop-off point. He
motioned the squad to stand and prepare to jump off from both sides
of the helicopter. The pilot hovered the helicopter 10 to 15 feet above the
river, and I thought I should jump first—lead by example. But I knew
that some squad members didn't swim well. I noticed that two squad
members had a death grip on the vertical poles inside the helicopter,
and their eyes were so wide they looked like cartoon characters. One
by one, I pried their fingers loose, pushed them off the helicopter, and
then jumped before the second squad member hit the water. Hitting
the water hard, I sank fast. I struggled to move upward until my head
popped above the surface, and I gasped for air. I swam toward them, but
they motioned that they were OK and dog-paddled toward shore. There
were multiple splashes behind me as the rest of the squad jumped and
hit the water. Once we'd swam to shore, the instructors had us form up
into a platoon formation to run back to the barracks.

Before our final training exercise, we had one more timed and graded
exercise—the river raft training. The squad, with packs and M1 rifles,
ran and carried the ten-man raft to the river. We paddled to a location
indicated by map coordinates. Once we hit land, the squad picked up
the raft and carried it for a distance across rough terrain to another
location in the river. Then we dropped the raft into the water, boarded,
and went to the next assigned location. We repeated the land-and-river
movement four or five times.

On one leg, we got to the riverbank and readied to launch the raft.
Wayne jumped in, swung his paddle around, and accidentally hit the

French instructor square in the mouth, knocking out a front tooth. We saw the blood dripping from his mouth. At first, I thought a fight would break out between Wayne and the instructor, but it de-escalated as fast as it had started. This instructor's facial expression displayed displeasure with Wayne, and I believe he had it in for him for the rest of the course.

Venturing miles into the Black Forest for our last three days of school, the platoon had day and night missions, including ambushes and raids. The lessons previously learned in getting through obstacle courses and land navigation applied in maneuvering the squads in the mountainous region. We were in our element now. The platoon ambushed the French soldiers when they were setting up ambushes for us, and we evaded their attempts to find us. As in many other training exercises, I found it difficult walking in the dense forest. My mind wandered to my days in Vietnam, walking point and looking for enemy ambushes and booby traps, and I did the same in this training. My body and mind stayed in the fight-or-flight mode, even though I knew it was a training exercise and that there was no real danger.

The first day, we walked through the rough terrain and thick forest. In the late afternoon, I was in the rear of the squad when they stopped. I moved forward to find Wayne sitting on the ground.

Standing over Wayne, I asked, "What's wrong?"

"I quit!" he replied.

I yelled, "Wayne, get your ass up, and let's go!"

"If I could get up, I would whip your ass," he replied with anger. "I can't walk in these boots."

"Take them off, and I'll trade you," I replied.

He'd traded his boots earlier for a brand-new pair of French boots. His feet had blisters. I took off my boots, gave them to Wayne, and slid my feet into his boots; we wore the same size. I picked up his pack and gear and carried it for him. We needed to finish as a squad. I figured I owed him for the boxing matches.

The first night, we sat around, preparing our c-rations for our dinner meal, when I heard a helicopter approaching with the distinct sound of the blades hitting the air—*Whop! Whop! Whop!*—that I'd heard many times in Vietnam. The helicopter landed in the small clearing, and several French soldiers jumped off, carrying what looked like a folding table and chairs. They ran over to where the instructors were sitting and set up the table and chairs, put a tablecloth on the table, and placed plates, flatware, food, and wine on the table. The soldiers jumped back onto the helicopter; it lifted, banked right, and disappeared over the tree line. The instructors were ready for their dinner meal. Later that evening, the helicopter and soldiers returned to pick up the items they'd left for the instructor's dinner. The next day, Wayne got his gear, but he kept my boots. We finished as a squad.

When the exercise ended, we loaded into the trucks for the ride back to post. We showered and changed into our Khaki uniforms for graduation. The Commandant officially recognized us as Commandos, and we received the French Commando Badge and Certificate. One soldier in the platoon did not graduate because of an injury, but there were no quitters. My squad members and the rest of the platoon were outstanding soldiers, didn't complain, and worked well together to complete the course.

Married platoon members' families attended the graduation ceremony. We'd found the course challenging, but now, we were glad we'd graduated and were going home. The platoon rode back to Heilbronn in the back of the trucks, with our wives and children following by car.

We received special orders from the Department of the Army recognizing the

Figure 3–1 Wayne Haynie on an obstacle at the French Commando Course, May 1974. (Photographer Unknown)

French Commando Badge as a foreign award. We wore the badge above the right breast pocket of our Dress Green uniform, the designated location for wearing foreign awards.

After Wayne got back from the French Commando Course, Dee went into labor. On June 13, 1974, she delivered a baby boy. Wayne and Dee had a neighbor care for Traci when they went to the Army hospital in Stuttgart. He was healthy, and the delivery proceeded with no problems. They named him after Wayne, and everyone called him "Little Wayne." Even though he towers over me today, I still call him "Little Wayne."

Figure 3–2 My squad at French Commando Course, May 1974 (it's all about teamwork). Photographer unknown.

TIME TO LEAVE

In the middle of July 1974, Wayne, Dee, Paula, and I took a three-day weekend to go to the military resort area in Berchtesgaden. Wayne had bought a used Ford sedan not long after he got in-country, and it had plenty of room for the luggage and the eight of us. We took David, John, Traci, and Little Wayne—at four weeks old—on the trip. We drove

Figure 3–3 My squad at French Commando Course, May 1974. French instructor sitting up front, and Wayne squatting, first in the second row. Another French instructor in middle rear, wearing a beret.

for three hours and arrived in the late afternoon. After we checked in, I found the rooms to be ordinary but not expensive.

Vacationing at Armed Forces Recreation Center (AFRC) Europe facilities in southern Bavaria is one benefit of duty in Europe. At the Chiemsee Recreation Center, The Lake Hotel actually sat on the edge of the 64-acre Lake Chiemsee. The resort was in southern Bavaria. Hitler had chosen this site for the first rest house of the Autobahn system and had built a large Rasthaus complex on the shore of the lake. The complex opened in 1938. It served its original purpose for a few years but was con-verted to a hospital during World War II. We found The Park Hotel in the woods, a short distance away from the lake. It was a stunning resort, with thick, green forests and mountains in the backdrop. Along with offering affordable accom-modations, the facilities offered an English-speaking staff, American-style dining rooms and dancing in the in-house club.

I thought it great to get away from the Company and its problems, which had not gone away when we came

Figure 3–4 French Commando Badge awarded after successful completion of the three-week course, May 1974. The number "4" on the badge represents the specific school we attended.

Figure 3–5 Left to Right - Wayne Haynie and I sitting by the lake at Chiemsee, relaxing, July 1974. Photographer Dee Haynie.

back from the French Commando Course. Being in Chiemsee with Wayne and our wives felt like another world. We spent our time dining and dancing, and we had plenty of time for sitting around and talking. I don't believe we left the resort area during the entire three days. We relaxed.

It wasn't long after finishing French Commando School that Paula told me we were expecting our third baby in early March 1975. The due date could either create a problem for us or get us home earlier. She couldn't fly after seven months of pregnancy, so we needed to leave early or stay longer to meet that requirement. I submitted to leave December 15 instead of the actual date of January 15 or a late March date. The Command approved my request. In early December, we had the movers pack and crate our belongings and transport them back to the United States. I shipped my car, too. We stayed with Wayne and Dee for two weeks until we caught our flight out of Frankfurt.

Wayne drove Paula, David, John, and me to the Frankfurt International Airport to catch our flight home. He pulled into the unloading area, and we all got out of the car. Paula held onto the boys while Wayne and I unloaded the car. We said our goodbyes and hugged. Then he got into the car and drove away, heading back to Heilbronn. We went inside the terminal, to the military desk. The sergeant looked at my orders and told me we were three days early. I wasn't happy.

We'd received an inaccurate departure date, so we stayed in Frankfurt for three more days. I called the executive officer, Lieutenant Burleson, at the Company, and he said he couldn't get the date changed. The four of us stayed in one room on post near the airport, waiting for our departure date. Paula stayed in the room while I took the boys to the cafeteria to eat breakfast and lunch; I brought food back for her. We went as a family to the cafeteria for the dinner meal. We played games with David and John to keep them entertained. The boys behaved themselves but needed room to run and play, but it was too cold and wet to go outside, so the hallway became their playground. The three days of being cooped up and waiting became frustrating.

On the fourth day, we boarded our flight and flew to Columbus, Georgia, with both boys. David and John were good travelers and were well behaved on the trip. We stayed at my parents' house until I got our car from the port at Charleston, South Carolina. My dad drove me to Charleston and then followed me back to Columbus.

The Army assigned me to the 101st Airborne Division, another light-infantry unit. Fort Campbell spans the Kentucky-Tennessee border between Hopkinsville, Kentucky, and Clarksville, Tennessee. Fort Campbell, named after Brigadier General William Bowen Campbell, a Union Army officer, is home to the 101st Airborne Division. I contacted John Lee and let him know the day and time we would arrive. John had been assigned to the 101st six months earlier.

My three years in Germany were disappointing. The promise that Germany was *the* place to soldier no longer rang true. My experiences with the soldiers from the draft years, during the Vietnam War, the drug and alcohol abuse, and the racial tension tested every leadership skill I could muster, but it didn't satisfy the need of soldiering.

I thought of soldiering as being with the platoon members I'd served with in Vietnam, First Platoon. To me, soldiering was the Brotherhood, working together for a common cause, being respectful of each other, and knowing the soldier next to you was technically and tactically proficient. The platoon members trusted and depended on one another because their life depended on it. They ignored the faults of others and were selfless with their knowledge and their own safety. My First Platoon brothers showed up for me every day. This was missing in my infantry unit in Germany. These past three years, there were NCOs and officers who'd mentored me. I'd learned from them, and, for that, I was grateful. I became a better NCO and person because of them. Another positive from my time in Germany was no protesters. German citizens didn't care if I served in Vietnam or not. The only negative comment about my Vietnam service was from officers, NCOs, and soldiers who called me a "baby killer" because of the Americal Division insignia I wore. They thought of it as joking, but it still offended me. My time in

Germany would be my worst experience while serving in the Army, and I knew I didn't want to go back.

December 1974—I'm 24 years old, married, with two children, and leaving for my fourth assignment after six years and five months of service.

CHAPTER 4

FORT CAMPBELL, KENTUCKY

"They have us surrounded. The poor bastards!"
~ 101ST AIRBORNE TROOPER AT BASTOGNE, BELGIUM, 1944.

In early January 1975, Sergeant First Class John Lee, my mentor from Germany, stood waiting as we drove through the main gates of Fort Campbell. John used his contact, the Battalion Command Sergeant Major, and had me assigned to his platoon. The replacement detachment had my orders to the 2nd Platoon Alpha Company 1st Battalion/506th Infantry Regiment 2nd Brigade 101st Airborne Division (Air Assault). I moved the car to a parking space to the right of the Military Police guard shack, located between the roads entering and exiting post, and got out as John approached the car. We shook hands, and he said "Hello" to Paula and the boys. I'd missed John and was happy to see him again. I followed John to the replacement center to sign in and report to my unit. The NCO at the Replacement Company told me I'd be at Fort Campbell for five years. With that information, Paula and I bought a house instead of renting.

Owning a home in the Army is a risky venture. The Army moved a soldier, on average, every two years, and sometimes he received orders three months or less before his reporting date. If he owns a home, it's his responsibility to rent or sell his home before moving. The soldier doesn't have a choice to move or not move. The Army provided no help in selling or renting his home, as corporations did. The Army shipped his household goods and furniture and paid mileage and per diem for the number of travel days and distance from his current location to his new assignment. I hoped we would be at Fort Campbell for five years.

We stayed in guest housing, Army hotel, on post until we found a place to live. I thought of buying a house in John's neighborhood. But it was an older neighborhood, and I preferred a new home. Within a week, we found a new home 15 minutes from post, a white brick one-story house with three bedrooms, two bathrooms, living room, eat-in kitchen, and a large one-car garage, around 1500 square feet. We purchased the house for $28,800. Within several weeks, we were moving in, had our furniture delivered, and were organizing our new home. David and John liked the big yard we had. On weekends, David and I picked up the hundreds of rocks the builder had left in the yard. We used his red wagon to carry the loads, and we dumped them in the woods behind the house. During my assignment with the 101st, I seldom drank—the first time in years I'd abstained.

REPORTING FOR DUTY

I reported to my platoon, and John introduced me to everyone. He assigned me as the weapons squad leader. The only difference between this weapons squad and the weapons squad in Germany was that this one had tube-launched, optically tracked, wire-guided systems (TOW) assigned. The TOW is an anti-tank missile tripod, helicopter or vehicle mounted. I needed to break out the manuals and learn this system. The weapons squad members, good soldiers, took an interest in their job and appeared proficient. The other squad leaders welcomed me to the platoon.

The Company had formations each morning for physical training and to pass out any necessary information. We had physical training Monday, Wednesday, and Friday mornings. We did calisthenics and a four-mile run in less than 32 minutes. I ran another two to three miles each evening after we got the kids to bed.

I soon learned that drug and racial problems didn't exist in this unit. Soldiers returning late from weekend passes became the biggest discipline problem. Within a month, I'd heard every excuse in the book for getting back to the squad late. I could live with this problem—this was night and day, compared to Germany. In July 1973 the draft ended, and most of the soldiers assigned to the Company were volunteers. The Vietnam War ended in 1975. Both were major events in our country's history, but I believed the war ending was the most important factor. I woke in the mornings excited about going to work. There was so much less stress with this unit.

We had training exercises, like we had in Germany, but we used helicopters to move us from one location to another. But the oil embargo that caused the 1973–1975 recession reduced flight time for helicopters, and there were budget constraints. There were times we used 2½ ton trucks to simulate helicopters landing at a Landing Zone for training. Putting gas into a truck was cheaper than a helicopter.

After the Vietnam War ended in 1975, the Army instituted a Reduction in Force (RIF). Civilians call it "layoffs," and every Company Commander in the Battalion left the Army, released from active duty. Officers weren't the only ones affected. NCOs and soldiers who had an average or marginal rating couldn't re-enlist, and they were released from active duty. The Department of Defense deactivated units to reduce the size of the Army and cut costs. With the reduction in force, there were budget shortfalls that led to involuntary extensions of overseas tours. Wayne had his tour in Germany extended by three months. I felt sorry for him. He wouldn't return to the States until April 1976 instead of January 1976. Soldiers on short tours—one year—received a one-month extension. The Army said extensions were necessary to overcome shortages of permanent change of station (PCS) travel funds due to the rising costs of transportation. This extension affected morale, and I'm sure soldiers left the Army because of it.

On March 3, 1975, Paula went into labor with Brooke, my new daughter. We coordinated earlier with John and his wife to care for David and John, whom we dropped off on the way to the hospital. Then I took Paula to the Army hospital and checked her into the maternity ward. After the doctor examined Paula, a nurse told me to go home, and she'd call when the time came. She asked if I'd attended the training to allow me to be in the delivery room, and I responded "No." Either no one had told me about this choice or it wasn't available in Germany. She looked at me and said I looked like a strong, well-adjusted sergeant and that she'd let me witness the birth of Brooke. I thought, *That's an experience I don't want to miss.*

I went home and fell asleep right away. An hour after I'd fallen asleep, the phone rang waking me. I mumbled "Hello" into the receiver; it was the nurse, telling me to come back to the hospital. I dressed and drove to the hospital. The nurse had me wash my hands and dressed me in a gown over my clothes. I had to wear a face mask. Paula lay stretched out, with knees in the air, on a hospital bed in the delivery room; the nurse had me stand at the head of the bed, so I didn't get to see the actual birth of my daughter. She came out crying and fighting, and the nurse said it was a healthy baby girl. Paula and I were excited to have a girl. I had named none of my sons after me, so I named my new daughter Glynda Brooke Haynie, thinking it fitting she carry my name. Paula called her Brooke, which was disappointing.

After being assigned to the platoon for two months, John Lee got orders to attend the Infantry Advanced Noncommissioned Officer Course (ANCOC), a demanding 12-week course at Fort Benning, Georgia, and one of the first courses for senior NCOs. A board at the Department of Army selected NCOs with the pay grade E7 and select E6s to attend, a competitive selection process. John had me take over the platoon while he attended school for three months. I became the platoon sergeant while John trained at Fort Benning. I performed well as the platoon sergeant, and the only problem was figuring out who was best at any given task we encountered, knowing the leaders and soldiers of the platoon. The squad leaders supported me and helped me learn my new position.

We had training exercises during his absence. The platoon loaded into helicopters for a combat assault, with the sound of Huey rotors hitting the air, and then jumped off the helicopter once we landed in the landing zone. This awoke hidden memories in me. I thought I'd locked those memories away. I still repeated the names of the platoon members killed every day but no longer ran the mental video of those days. The video replayed often while I was with the 101st. During this time, I started writing a book about my experiences in Vietnam but, within months, gave up the effort.

WEEK OF THE EAGLES

Within weeks of John returning to the platoon, the Division had the Week of the Eagles. The main purpose of the Week of the Eagles was to help honor the Soldiers of the 101st and Fort Campbell. During the Week of the Eagles, we took part in the unit competition, military skills, and sports, within the division. I would wake up with anticipation and excitement for the upcoming competition. As I lay in bed, the sun was just rising over the horizon, and its light was trickling into the bedroom. Watching the sunlight moving across the floor closer and closer to me, I thought of my platoon brothers who didn't come home from Vietnam and repeated their names: "Tufts, Ramos, Reynolds, Ofstedahl, Swindle, Wellman, Ponce, Mitchell, Anderson, Carey, Morris, Kidwell, and Matson." After I said the last name and his face disappeared, I rolled out of bed to get ready for the big day.

I trained and got the TOW gunners ready for the competition. We didn't take first place, but I was proud of the TOW team's performance. I thought we did well for me not having any experience with the TOW before coming to Fort Campbell. Another event, the 25-mile run in uniform and boots, wearing my helmet, backpack, canteen with water, and M16 rifle challenged me.

We started the run in platoon formation, but by the five-mile mark, many platoon members had slowed and others had sped up, so the formation no longer existed. I ran among other soldiers who were not in my platoon, and many times I thought of dropping out of the run as I passed many soldiers sitting along the road, quitting the run and some being treated by medics. A Lieutenant pulled up and ran alongside me and made the statement that NCOs couldn't make it to the finish line. Then he moved ahead of me at a faster pace. That gave me the motivation I needed. I completed the run wearing bloody boots in four hours and thirty-five minutes. I couldn't go to work the next day because of the bloody blisters on my feet, and I couldn't pull my boots on over my swollen feet. Hell, I couldn't move, I was so sore!

After the Week of the Eagles, the Battalion Command Sergeant Major assigned me to work in Operations (S3) and become the assistant operations NCO for the Battalion. The Battalion Operations is responsible for training and creates a list of tasks to grade individual and unit performance during training exercises. During deployment, they write the Standard Operating Procedures (SOP) for combat situations and provide After Action Reports to the Commander. The new job excited me—it was something I'd never done. Although I was no longer in John's platoon, we remained friends.

TRAINING NATIONAL GUARD SOLDIERS

Training National Guard soldiers would be another new and challenging task. We were preparing to leave for Camp McCoy, Wisconsin, to train the Wisconsin and Ohio National Guard units for a month. Camp McCoy is in Wisconsin, between the two cities of Sparta and Tomah. The Army used it primarily as a military training center.

One of my main duties was to track the units—the Battalion and the two guard units with support units—enter their locations on the maps, and then brief the Battalion Commander each morning. I'd use my map-reading skills but needed to learn unit symbols and the correct method for drawing them on the map overlays. Fortunately, I found everything I needed in a manual. The unit moved out by convoy, driving north along Interstate 57 for most of the trip. I rode in a car with John and two other NCOs from the platoon to Camp McCoy.

While driving around Chicago, I noticed the traffic moving at a high rate of speed, reminding me of the Autobahn in Germany. Sitting behind the driver, I looked out the passenger window and saw a family cruising along the highway. A young boy and I made eye contact; I smiled at him, and he smiled and waved. A second after he waved, a car that was following us changed lanes and bumped that family's car. I watched in horror as the car, doing 65 miles an hour, flipped over, and I saw the terror in the young boy's eyes. I yelled for the driver to stop as I looked out the rear window and saw the car rolling two more times. But he couldn't stop—there were too many cars speeding by us. I never found out what happened to that family. The trip took around 11 hours of driving time to get to Camp McCoy.

Once we arrived, the advance-party NCOs told us where our quarters were. John and the other two NCOs joined their platoons, and I found the barracks. The room, a standard Army barracks room 10 by 8 feet, white walls, grey linoleum flooring, with a steel gray bunk and mattress. Two wall lockers lined one wall, and the far wall had a window. I found a pillow with a pillowcase, two white sheets and a green woolen blanket folded and stacked at the foot of the bunk.

I put my gear away, changed into my uniform, and reported to the Battalion headquarters. Once there, I set my maps up with acetate overlays taped to the board so I could flip the overlay to show different detail information about the unit locations. The units called in their grid coordinates whenever they moved to a new location. I took this information and erased the old position on the map. Then, using a grease pencil, I'd draw the correct symbol for their new position. There were many infantry and support units reporting that required updates. The Battalion Commander used this information to move units. It wasn't unusual for the Battalion Commander or the Command Sergeant Major to want multiple briefings during the day.

When not updating the maps, I helped the Operations NCO make changes and updates to the training schedule we used during the exercise. Then we relayed the changes to the units affected. A change could be the time of day for a unit to be on a range for live-fire exercises or changing the scheduled location of one of our platoons to help in training. I answered radio and telephone calls and passed messages to the right staff person for action. It might appear I didn't have enough work, but I stayed busy.

During the evenings we were off unless the Battalion scheduled a night exercise, and we were free on several weekends during the training. John and I went to downtown Madison and visited the main strip. Getting something to eat and then hitting a club for a few drinks became our typical weekend. We never stayed out too late.

While at Camp McCoy, I learned how battalion operations functioned during this exercise. The two National Guard units performed satisfactorily, but the troops appeared lazy or like they didn't care about learning. These soldiers reinforced the regular Army stereotype of the National Guard units not being professional. Our NCOs helped in the training, and our troops played the part of enemy soldiers against the guard units. Our Battalion troops performed outstandingly, and I was proud to be part of the Battalion.

The time flew by while I was at Camp McCoy, and I enjoyed my new position. Working in Operations had its challenges, and I found it interesting to learn how an Infantry Battalion performed its missions, but I found it not as challenging, rewarding, or exciting as being in an Infantry Company with troops. I joined John and the two other NCOs for the trip back home. We had an uneventful return trip, and I found it great to be back home and at Fort Campbell.

INFANTRY ADVANCE NCO COURSE

I received orders for ANCOC after being back home a month from training at Camp McCoy. When I received the notification to attend ANCOC, Battalion had slated me to attend the Air Assault School and the Pathfinder School, with a two-week break between the two courses at Fort Campbell. Because ANCOC had priority over the other two courses, I wouldn't have the opportunity to attend the Air Assault or Pathfinder schools while at Fort Campbell.

Being selected as an E6 to attend the Infantry ANCOC, the same three-month course John had attended earlier, was an accomplishment. The course had both classroom instruction and practical-application classes in the field. The course curriculum split the classroom and field-training time equally. We learned leadership, light-infantry and mechanized tactical operations, air-assault operations, Nuclear Chemical and Biological Warfare, land navigation, and many other topics. We conducted physical training three days a week and took the APFT before graduation.

I reported to Fort Benning, Georgia, for the Infantry Advance NCO Course. We received Field Manuals and a weekly training schedule for the three months. It was our responsibility to make the morning formations and attend the training each day. I found the formation humorous because so many different kinds of odd headgear were worn in the early '70s by different units. There were maroon berets (82nd Airborne Division), blue berets (101st Airborne Division, Air Assault), black berets (Ranger), green berets (Special Forces), Drill Sergeant hat, Cavalry hats (1st Cavalry Division), and the standard-issue green baseball hat. Anyone not in the Army would think that soldiers from different services and countries made up the men in the formation.

I stayed at my parents' house, in my old bedroom, instead of the barracks. We hadn't been back to visit for seven months. Paula and the kids went to stay at her mom's house in Albany, Georgia. Staying at her mom's would be closer to Fort Benning than leaving them at Fort Campbell, and I tried to visit on weekends when possible. Living in my old bedroom brought back memories of my youth, not as a kid but as a young soldier going to Vietnam and coming back from an unpopular war. While living there, I thought more often of the 13 platoon brothers who didn't come home.

ANCOC was a demanding course but not too difficult; it reinforced much of the knowledge I had gained being assigned to infantry units the last seven years. I studied each night to prepare for the next day's lessons. Each morning I awoke early—5:00 AM—drove the 15 minutes to Fort Benning, did physical training, and attended classes. Several weeks, we went to the field for two or three days to practice and reinforce what we'd learned in the classroom.

I'd been attending the course for around a month when one morning I heard my father vomiting in his bathroom. This wasn't unusual during his drinking days, but he hadn't taken a drink in two years. I got up to check if he was OK and saw him vomiting blood into a wastebasket; the wastebasket was half full of blood. I told him he needed to go to the hospital, now. I found my mother in the kitchen. I told her what was happening and then drove them both to the hospital. After an examination, the doctor admitted dad and sent him to surgery. He was bleeding internally from his esophagus. The doctor told mom and me that he wouldn't survive because his many years of drinking had eroded his esophagus. I called the course First Sergeant, and he told me to take the time I needed. I then notified the Red Cross to get Wayne home from Germany.

While dad was in surgery, the hospital put out a call to the units on Fort Benning for soldiers to donate blood for my dad. He was losing blood faster than the doctors could pump it back into his body. Shortly after the call went out, I took the elevator downstairs to the lab and found a line of more than 75 soldiers waiting to donate blood. I walked along the line and thanked the soldiers for helping my father. I believe these soldiers who donated blood saved his life.

When dad came out of surgery in a coma, the doctors didn't expect him to live. I made many phone calls to the Red Cross to find out where Wayne was, and the Red Cross didn't know. With no notification from the Red Cross, it took several days for Wayne to get home, and he called me when he arrived. I picked Wayne up at the airport and was happy to see him again but wished our visit could have been under other circumstances. Mom contacted dad's brother, Jack, and told him he needed to come to the hospital. Jack flew in from Virginia, and I picked him up at the airport. He departed the plane drunk and asked me not to tell my mother. I didn't need to tell her.

While waiting to see if Dad was going to live or die, Wayne and I talked about our days growing up with an Army father. There was no denying his drinking and devotion to the Army had created a problem within the family. But there were times he took us fishing, in particular when we lived in Virginia, and cheered us on when attending our Little League baseball games while in Orleans, France. Living at Fort Benning, we went boating and fishing at the Chattahoochee River Reservoir, and he coached our baseball team at the Boys Club for several years. Bowling was always a good family outing. Although he didn't hug us or say, "I love you," I believe he loved us in his own way.

Figure 4–1 My father, John W. Haynie. Photograph taken March 1965, four years before he retired.

He served in World War II as a 19-year-old and landed on the beaches of Anzio, and, later in his career, in 1967, he, too, served in Vietnam. I'm sure both wars changed his life, and he had his own fear he carried that he needed to control. Dad did well in his career, being promoted to E7 Master Sergeant, the highest enlisted rank at the time, and then taking a promotion to Warrant Officer and several years later being commissioned as a Captain. These were great achievements for a kid with a high school diploma from the mountains of North Carolina.

I went to class and back to the hospital whenever the doctors said they needed me there. One morning, while in the field, I jumped up with my classmates to board a helicopter for a combat-assault exercise, when a cadre NCO came over and told me I needed to go to the hospital. I went back and forth many times in order to continue the rest of the course. There were many times I would go to school to take an exam with my classmates, without having attending the classes, and then return to the hospital. Dad came home when I had two weeks left in the course. He recovered and lived another nine years after the doctors said he had three years to live.

The cadre at the Advance Course treated me with respect, and they worked with me to give me the time I needed. I learned from the First Sergeant how important respect, taking care of your soldiers, and compassion were as leadership traits. I graduated with my class and was designated an Honor Graduate. To this day, I don't know how I balanced studying and staying at the hospital. Paula and the kids met me at my parents' house, and we drove back to Fort Campbell after my graduation.

NEW ASSIGNMENT

We were back at Fort Campbell less than two weeks when I received orders for Drill Sergeant duty at Fort Jackson, South Carolina, with a report date of January 3, 1976. Paula and I put the house up for sale and were lucky; it sold in the first week, and we made a little profit. We moved to a rental a mile from our house until we left Fort Campbell in mid-December 1975, heading for Fort Jackson.

In Germany, I'd traded my 1970 Camaro for a 1972 Ford Mustang right before I'd left and shipped the Mustang home. In late 1975, I sold the Mustang and bought a Dodge cargo van. I needed more room for the kids. In the mid-'70s, converting a cargo van for family use became popular. John and I worked weekends converting the inside of the van with wood paneling, seats, a bench that held cargo, and an audio system with speakers. We covered the floor with quality indoor-outdoor carpet, easy to keep clean. I didn't own or use tools, but John had tools and was good with them. We took three weekends to complete the conversion. We had a great time working together. John and I took breaks, talked, and had family lunches and dinners together during these weekends. I couldn't have done this on my own. It became a standing joke in my house that, if I entered a room holding a tool, everyone asked me to stop and explain what repair or project I planned on using the tool for. I wasn't to be trusted.

When it came time for us to leave Fort Campbell, we met John and his wife and said our goodbyes. He'd received orders for Drill Sergeant duty, too, but to Fort Dix, New Jersey. I wouldn't see John Lee again. I packed the van with what we needed for the trip and got the family loaded. We drove off to Columbus first for a visit and then to Fort Jackson.

Fort Jackson, named after Andrew Jackson, the seventh President of the United States and a former Army General. It is primarily an Army Training and Doctrine Command (TRADOC) installation, which operates Basic Combat Training (BCT) and is located in Columbia, South Carolina.

My year at Fort Campbell met most of my expectations about soldiering. Under the leadership of Sergeant First Class John Lee, I'd enjoyed my time with the soldiers, NCOs, and officers of the 101st Airborne Division. Performing as a squad leader and platoon sergeant, and working in the Battalion operations challenged me, and it was rewarding. I wish my assignment would've been longer than one year.

December 1975—I'm 25 years old, married, with three children, and leaving for my fifth assignment after seven years and five months of service.

CHAPTER 5

DRILL SERGEANT DUTY

"This Is My Rifle, This Is My Gun"

I arrived at Fort Jackson, South Carolina, on January 5, 1976, with Paula, David, John, and Brooke. Family quarters wouldn't be available for 30 days, so until quarters became available, we rented an apartment that was a ten-minute drive from the Company Headquarters. The next stop was to sign in for my new assignment.

I reported to the Replacement Company for in-processing to Fort Jackson. I approached the desk of the closest clerk and handed him a copy of my orders. He looked at my orders and then at some papers on his desk and said, "Your orders are changed from the 2nd Basic Training Brigade to the 5th Basic Training Brigade."

I asked, "Why the change, and what is the 5th Brigade?"

"The Brigade is short Drill Sergeants, and to answer your second question, it's an all-female Brigade," he replied while flashing a big smile.

I didn't see the humor and asked, "Are you sure this isn't a mistake on my assignment?"

"No mistake," he replied.

He handed me a copy of my new orders, and it stated my assignment was the 5th Brigade. I left the Replacement Company confused and trying to figure out how I would get out of reporting to the 5th Brigade. After thinking it through, I knew I wasn't going to get out of this assignment.

That afternoon, I reported to the 5th Training Brigade, the all-female Brigade. The Women's Army Corps (WAC) still existed in 1976. The Battalion Commander, Sergeant Major, Company Commander, and First Sergeant were female; my chain of command consisted of female officers and NCOs. Drill Sergeants, supply clerks, and cooks were the only males in the Battalion. I believe that, in my entire Army career to this point, I had ever seen a female soldier, not counting nurses and, recently, several administrative soldiers. Female soldiers were a foreign concept to this infantryman.

I entered the Battalion Commander's office, where Lieutenant Colonel Gibson sat behind her large desk, a small, older woman with many streaks of gray running through her short, dark hair, and I stopped several steps in front of her desk, stood at attention, saluted, and said, "Ma'am, Sergeant Haynie reports."

Staying seated, she returned my salute and said, "At Ease."

I lowered my salute and assumed the "At Ease" position, feet apart with hands behind my back.

The Lieutenant Colonel smiled and asked, "Sergeant Haynie, what do you think of being assigned to the 5th Brigade?"

"Ma'am, I came here to train soldiers, not women. I want a transfer to another Brigade," I blurted out without thinking of the consequences of my statement.

The Colonel's smile disappeared as her eyes narrowed, and she called me to the position of attention and told me that, in no uncertain terms, I'd train soldiers. Then she dismissed me. Without a word, I saluted, executed an about-face, and walked out of her office. I hadn't planned on making that statement; it came out without me thinking.

This wasn't a good start in the Battalion. I didn't have much contact with the Battalion Commander after this meeting, but I'm sure she followed my progress as a Drill Sergeant.

I reported to my Company Commander and First Sergeant after meeting with the Battalion Commander, and there was no mention of my statement to her. I'm sure the Battalion Commander had told them what I said, but, this time, I kept my thoughts to myself. The First Sergeant assigned me to a platoon to tag along for a training cycle. I had to wear a black polished helmet liner, like I did on the range at Fort Benning, to identify me as cadre. The drill sergeants called anyone who wears a helmet liner a "turtle." I couldn't wait to go to the Drill Sergeant Academy.

This would be my first assignment not working with only Infantry NCOs, and I found many of the Drill Sergeants in the Company hadn't served in Vietnam. This doesn't mean they weren't good NCOs, but they had a different mindset from an Infantry NCO who'd served in Vietnam. Something was missing, but nothing I could put my finger on, to identify the difference.

After a month, February 1976, with the basic training platoon, the First Sergeant sent me to the Instructor Training Course (ITC), a two-week course. The Instructor Training Course taught me how to present instruction, the Army way, and how to prepare a lesson plan. I found the course easy and did well. I graduated as a Distinguished Graduate when I completed the course. When I got back to the unit, the First Sergeant told me I'd attend the Drill Sergeant Academy in April.

In February 1976, Paula and I decided that our marriage wouldn't work. As in any marriage, we had a multitude of problems, and, out of respect, I won't discuss them here. I know the hours I worked and the time away from the family played a part in our decision. My assignments in Germany and Fort Campbell had me away from home as many days as I was home. And now I would become a Drill Sergeant working 12 to 14 hours a day, seven days a week. I don't know if getting married so soon after Vietnam had an impact or not; I guess Paula would be the only one able to answer that question. We stayed together until May, after I completed the Drill Sergeant Course. I had to live in the barracks during the four weeks of the course, and she could stay in quarters with the kids until I graduated.

LEARNING TO BE A DRILL SERGEANT

I found the Drill Sergeant Course competitive, challenging, and demanding, and the cadre posted the class standing by a numerical grade each week. We had graded examinations, and the cadre graded our daily performance. We gathered around the bulletin board each Friday evening to check our standing in the class.

My class lived in the barracks, and the cadre required us to keep our barracks, wall locker, footlocker, and bunk as a trainee did. I went home in the evenings to have supper with the family and study for classes for the next day and returned to the barracks to sleep before lights out. Dee and the kids returned home stateside after Wayne received a three-month involuntary extension in Germany. Dee, Traci, and little Wayne stayed with us for two weeks. In the evenings, Dee sat at the kitchen table and helped me study. For the practical work, I gave her drill commands, and she executed them, which made for realistic practice. I appreciated her patience and help. They moved to Fort Leonard Wood, Missouri, when Wayne returned from Germany.

We spent many hours on drill and ceremonies, rifle marksmanship and maintenance, nuclear, biological, and chemical warfare, physical training, and first aid, to name a few. These were the same subjects taught to trainees during basic training, and we learned how to present the material in an easy-to-understand method to trainees, which was more difficult than executing the action. The academy required us to memorize Field Manuals (FM), and two of the primary manuals used were the Drill and Ceremonies, FM-22–5, and Physical Training, FM 21–20.

Sergeant First Class Tweed had an assigned bunk next to my bunk, and our wall lockers stood side by side. He stood my height, was older by several years, and carried some extra pounds, but he was not overweight. He had a good personality, and nothing appeared to bother him. Tweed served in the medical field and didn't know soldiering, but he was a good NCO and a good person. I helped him organize his wall locker and footlocker, and, most mornings, I made his bunk for him. He had a hell of a time getting the corners angled correctly and the wool blanket tight enough to bounce a quarter into the air. Everything we learned applied to training trainees.

I competed against Staff Sergeant Wang for Distinguished Graduate going into the last week of training. He was an infantry NCO, six foot with a muscular build, short, light-brown hair, and he looked like a drill sergeant. We were even in points, and it was during the final inspection that the cadre selected him as the Distinguished Graduate and me as the Honor Graduate from our class. I thought second place a good achievement—no disappointment. We put on our Campaign Hat, Drill Sergeant Hat, and pinned our Drill Sergeant Badge centered on our right breast pocket of our uniform. I left the Academy proud of being a Drill Sergeant and graduating Honor Graduate.

Figure 5–1 Left to Right: Lieutenant Colonel Treadway and me receiving the award for Drill Sergeant Academy Honor Graduate, April 1976. The Colonel must be six foot five! Photographer unknown.

HISTORY OF THE CAMPAIGN HAT

BY DEPARTMENT OF ARMY

The current drill sergeant hat evolved from the 1883 campaign hat. That headgear was a modified (flat brim versus upturned brim) Montana Peak, which was adopted for wear by the army in 1911, and abandoned in 1942. In 1964, the hat was reintroduced to become a proud symbol of the drill sergeant.

The female drill sergeant hat came into being in 1972. It was designed by Brigadier General Mildred C. Bailey. The original design was taken from the Australian bush hat and was beige in color. In 1983, the color was changed to green with the style remaining unchanged.

The drill sergeants wear the campaign hat as a testament of their demonstrated professionalism, commitment to the mission, and proven leadership. The hat further symbolizes the lineage of the past, present, and future of the U.S. Army.

Figure 5–2 The US Army Drill Sergeant Hat; female hat on the left and male hat on right. The Drill Sergeant hat was worn after graduation from the Drill Sergeant Course. Photograph by Department of Army.

DRILL SERGEANT IDENTIFICATION BADGE

BY DEPARTMENT OF ARMY

Drill Sergeant Identification Badge—This We'll Defend

Prior to 1958, the badge was a regimental crest with a maroon background. In 1958, it was adopted as the training center's crest and the background was changed to green. All qualified drill sergeants wear the drill sergeant identification badge.

Each element of the badge has a specific meaning.

It consists of 13 stars representing the original colonies. The torch, burning brightly in the center, symbolizes liberty. The snake is derived from the original, "Don't Tread on Me" serpent, a symbol of American independence during the 18th century. Together with the torch and breastplate, it indicated readiness to defend. The breastplate is a symbol of strength. The green background is a vestment worn under the breastplate and called a Jupon, which represents the new Army. The snake grasps, with his tail and teeth, a scroll inscribed, "This We'll Defend."

Figure 5–3 The US Army Drill Sergeant Identification Badge, awarded after graduation from the Drill Sergeant Course. The badge was worn centered on the right breast pocket of the uniform. Photograph by Department of Army.

The inscription summarizes the meaning of all the symbols on the badge, depicting the determination, devotion, and constant readiness of the American Soldier.

After graduation, Paula and I separated and filed for divorce. She and the kids got an apartment across town, and she found a job near her apartment. I didn't take the divorce from Paula lightly. The reason wasn't important; it happened, and the divorce affected my children. I didn't spend enough time with them after the divorce but missed them more than I could ever explain. I let my career take priority over my children, and for that I'm sorry.

I got a two-bedroom apartment right outside the front gate of Fort Jackson, a five-minute drive to the Company. Tweed agreed to room with me, so we shared the apartment. The arrangement worked well because when I worked, he hung around the apartment on cycle break. We didn't see each other often but respected each other when we needed sleep. Sleep became important. I started drinking again and got back to drinking half a fifth a day. I did most of my drinking during cycle breaks, time off in between getting recruits, normally seven days. I don't think my drinking at this point was about Vietnam only, but a combination of the divorce, missing my kids, my work schedule, and thinking of my time in Vietnam. I was letting the stress of life get the best of me.

STILL LEARNING

The First Sergeant assigned me to 3rd platoon as the platoon sergeant after graduating, and I had a female drill sergeant, Sergeant Avery, as my assistant platoon sergeant. She already had two cycles under her belt. Sergeant Avery stood several inches shorter than me, physically fit and had short cropped brown hair under her Drill Sergeant Hat. I found her a good NCO and an excellent Drill Sergeant. We worked well together. The five platoons in the Company had a male platoon sergeant and a female assistant platoon sergeant.

We received new recruits days after I came back to the Company. I must confess my first training cycle wasn't a good one. Allowing the movies to influence me, I thought raising my voice at trainees would be effective. I soon learned it wasn't and did much better after that first training cycle, balancing all the leadership tools at my disposal and being myself. There is a time for discipline and a time for praise, and everyone gets both. Yes, there were times to raise my voice, but there were many more times to talk in an even tone. I learned that as a drill sergeant I couldn't let the "hat" make me into someone I'm not. The hat is a symbol of authority, discipline, and obedience, and is not to be taken lightly. I wore my Drill Sergeant Hat with pride and wanted to honor it the best I could.

During my first summer, second cycle, the First Sergeant attached several male drill sergeants, including me, to an all-male Company on Tank Hill. Most summers, the Army had an overload of males going on active duty, and the male training Battalions needed extra Drill Sergeants. I found the male trainees much more difficult to train than female trainees. The males were less interested in learning, appeared lazier, and spent more time arguing with each other than trying to work as a team. The female trainees learned, worked as a team, and wanted to be soldiers. To my amazement, I found the female trainee to be sloppy and dirty when it came to maintaining the barracks, and the male trainees were the opposite—they were neater and cleaner. Both male and female trainees had their challenges.

When people learned that I trained female soldiers, they asked if female trainees cried often and if they completed the physical requirements. Yes, I had female trainees cry, but I had male trainees cry, too. The female trainee cried because she couldn't complete a task or got too frustrated with a drill sergeant in her face. The male trainee cried because he wanted to quit and go home. And crying wasn't an everyday occurrence for either. A female, *on average*, couldn't run as fast or lift as much weight as a male trainee, but they passed the female requirements for physical training as did their male counterpart. Both had to pass all requirements for graduation; no one received a free pass.

Female soldiers had the same frustrations as male soldiers. I recall one evening after dinner, Sergeant Avery and I heard two trainees yelling profanities at each other. After each verbal exchange, they moved closer to each other, with their hands formed into a fist. We thought a fight would start, and Sergeant Avery moved in between the two trainees and ordered the one to her right to step back and stand at ease. She did as instructed. The other trainee, two inches taller than Sergeant Avery, 15 pounds heavier, and with arms a weightlifter would envy, turned her anger toward Sergeant Avery because of her frustration. She stepped forward with a threatening look on her face. It crossed my mind that she might whip Sergeant Avery's ass in front of the platoon. Hell, considering the size of the trainee, she might whip my ass! But Sergeant Avery moved toward her with her face around an inch away from the trainee's and the brim of her drill sergeant hat touching the trainee's forehead. In a low, steady voice, she told her to stand at ease. To our good fortune, she did. We knew no one's history and didn't take their past life for granted. I had the same situation with male trainees and handled it in the same manner without it becoming physical. A drill sergeant who believes they can whip anyone's ass because they wear the hat is making a grave mistake. We learned later that the smaller trainee wasn't staying in step while marching and that the larger trainee was correcting her, and, so, an argument had started between the two.

Besides the general comparison I've made here between male and female trainees, I want to add that the trainees entering the all-volunteer Army were good soldiers, regardless of gender, and didn't bring the baggage the draftees brought with them several years earlier. The soldiers I trained as a Drill Sergeant were far different from some of the soldiers I led in Germany. I didn't witness racial intolerance, nor did I see any drug use or disobedience of the orders given by an officer or NCO. Each platoon always had two or three trainees who had difficulty adjusting to the military and were given a Trainee Discharge, Honorable, and a few trainees each cycle received medical discharges, due to injuries or preexisting conditions, from the Army.

I took my duty as a Drill Sergeant seriously and wanted to make sure the trainees had the best possible training, in case they went to war. After my time in Vietnam, I understood the importance of training. Female trainees didn't go on to any combat arms training after basic. Basic training would be the only time they trained for small-unit tactics or firing weapons and the other basic skills needed in combat.

I knew from my combat experiences that training could save their life or a platoon member's life. If this attitude made me a hard ass, so be it.

After my third cycle, the Battalion Commander moved me from Delta Company to Echo Company; they were short several drill sergeants. Echo Company drill sergeants were excellent NCOs, too. I reported to Sergeant First Class Lake, the Senior Drill Sergeant, a six-foot, powerfully built black man, a robust and older airborne soldier. He briefed me on the Company and assigned me to my platoon. He was the most patient leader I had met. That is one trait I was still working on but was getting better in, because of Sergeant First Class Lake and working with trainees.

A DAY ON THE TRAIL

Being a drill sergeant meant I worked day and night for nine weeks. We called our Drill Sergeant Duty "being on the trail." My day started by waking at 4:00 AM, getting ready for work and then driving to post. The CQ had the trainees up and doing their morning routine: making their bunks, cleaning the barracks and latrine, and getting their gear ready for the training day before I arrived. We followed the training schedule, and I'd get home around 7:30 PM.

I ate my meals—breakfast, lunch, and supper—in the mess hall with the trainees, so I didn't do grocery shopping or cooking. Each evening I'd press my wash-and-wear fatigues while spraying them with starch, spit-shine my boots for the next day, and place my drill sergeant hat into a wood press overnight to keep the brim straight. I repeated the cycle every day for nine weeks. We worked most Saturdays and Sundays during those nine weeks, too. When they graduated, we got seven days off before the next platoon arrived and started the next nine weeks over again. It felt like the movie *Groundhog Day*. We joked that the trainee names were the same, but their faces were different each cycle.

When we first received our platoon of trainees, my assistant platoon sergeant and I would gauge each trainee's abilities and decided who would fill the trainee-leadership positions. We assigned four trainees as squad leaders and one trainee as the trainee platoon sergeant. They wore a black band on the left upper arm that had sergeant stripes sewed into the band. We dealt with the trainee leadership directly to carry out our orders to get the task done and give us fewer trainees to deal with; this saved time. We told the trainee leaders what needed to get done, and they told their fellow trainee squad members—no different from how an actual Army platoon leadership functioned.

One of the hardest tasks that I performed was showing the required placement of personal items, folding towels, washcloths, and other items, and how to hang their uniforms. We assigned each trainee a bunk, footlocker, and wall locker. Making the bunk and hanging the uniforms in the wall locker were easy tasks to explain, but the footlocker task I found more difficult at first. I showed where to store each item in the footlocker: personal items, toilet articles, underclothes, towels, and washcloths, to name a few. Showing the military method for folding each item made the task difficult for me. Here is an infantry soldier, a combat veteran, sitting at a selected trainee's footlocker, showing how to fold bras and panties. But I did this task instead of assigning my female assistant Drill Sergeant. This gave me the opportunity to show the trainees their treatment in the Army wouldn't be different because they were female soldiers.

I selected the trainee by her bust size. Now, this may sound crude or sexist, but there was a reason. I didn't want to show how to fold a bra with a big-busted trainee. I would most likely be too embarrassed. Nor would I choose a trainee who was small busted; she might be too embarrassed. So I picked a trainee, in my opinion, who was medium-sized. I stood over the bunk, holding her bra, and talked the platoon through each step as I folded the bra.

"You hold the bra and extend it in front of you, with the strap facing you, and then take the right cup and place it over the left cup, while sliding most of the strap between the two cups. The next step is to take the remaining strap and tuck it underneath the opening of the bottom cup so the strap and tag don't show. Now place the bra inside the top footlocker tray, right side, with the bottom of the cup facing front."

After I showed how to fold and display a bra, the panties were next. I used the same trainee to show how to fold panties.

"Lay the panties flat on a hard surface with the crotch centered and facing downward, and the seam toward you. Make sure the panties' left and right seams are even on each side. From the center, take the crotch and fold it upward, even with the waistband. Fold the left side of the panties to the center, and press with your hand. And then fold the right side over the left side, and press with your hand. Now place the panties inside the top footlocker tray, right side, with the folded side facing upward."

I found it awkward handling bras and panties for the demonstration, and it took several training cycles to get used to doing this task. I believe the trainees enjoyed my embarrassment at handling bras and panties.

On a typical training day, I arrived early in the morning, making sure the barracks met the standards and were clean, and then I had the platoon form up for the first formation of the day for physical training. Physical training included calisthenics and a run. We alternated which drill sergeant gave the physical training instruction each day. Whoever gave physical training stood on a platform in front of the Company formation of trainees at the physical-training field and led each exercise by naming the exercise, giving the starting-position command, and then counting the cadence and repetition for each exercise. The trainees echoed each repetition along with the Drill Sergeant. After the calisthenics, each platoon Drill Sergeant took their platoon for a run. Sometimes we formed into a Company formation for the morning run. The run lasted several miles and ended running up Tank Hill, a Fort Jackson landmark, which signaled the end of a long run up the installation's highest point. Several trainees from each platoon dropped out before reaching the top of the hill, the location of the water tower.

After the run, I marched the platoon to the mess hall for breakfast. I liked standing near the chow line for the meals and encouraged trainees to try foods that they never had at home. Shit on a Shingle (SOS) and grits were my two favorite breakfast foods to get trainees to eat. The cooks made SOS with white gravy and chipped or ground beef served over toast. It tasted better than it looked or the name suggested. Grits came from hominy, which is corn, and is a breakfast food in southern states. I admit it took a acquired taste and plenty of butter and cheese to like grits. The trainees' expressions while eating SOS or grits for the first time were priceless. The drill sergeants sat at a long table at the back of the mess hall. We talked about the daily schedule and went over our assignments; rifle marksmanship was today's training.

After chow, the Company drew their M16s from the arms room and formed up to take "cattle cars" to the rifle range. A "cattle car" in the Army was a truck with a trailer hitched to it used to transport soldiers to training sites. Units packed so many soldiers into the trailer that many had to stand, holding onto a pole or strap to keep their balance; there was no room for anyone to move. During the drive to the training site, my entertainment was watching trainees sound asleep, standing and holding onto a strap or pole, swaying with the movement of the cattle car. I believe the name "cattle car" derived from overloading the trailer with soldiers so that, like cattle, they slept standing during transport.

Once the Company unloaded from the trucks, the range cadre took charge of the trainees. The cadre presented classes on marksmanship and range safety. Then the trainees moved to the firing line. The Drill Sergeants were safety NCOs on the range, and I'd move along the firing line and make sure the trainees followed instructions and in the correct firing position; this day we used the prone firing position.

I stopped and stood straddled over a trainee to correct her body alignment behind the M16, as I had done many times earlier. As I touched her shoulder with my safety paddle to show where the butt of the rifle should sit, the weapon discharged. I rolled to my right, hitting the ground hard, and crawled, moving as fast as I could, away from the trainee. A weapon firing still bothered me, and a trainee firing a weapon bothered me more. When I realized no one was shooting at me, I jumped up and headed for the trainee with the full intention of strangling her. Sergeant First Class Lake jumped in between me and the trainee; he knew how

I'd react. He made me go to the range building and take a break so I wouldn't hurt the trainee. My reaction to a trainee firing their weapon by accident didn't differ from any other Drill Sergeant's. A trainee with a loaded weapon is a dangerous trainee—hell, a trainee with a weapon is a dangerous trainee, period.

While the trainees were on the firing line, the cooks set up a hot meal for the Company on a line of wooden picnic tables, and we stopped at noon for an hour lunch. The other Drill Sergeants took this opportunity to harass me regarding the trainee who'd fired her weapon. I didn't see the humor. After lunch, the training continued.

When a trainee finished firing their weapon and left the firing line, they did a left or right face, depending on their position to the center of the range. Then they walked single file toward the two drill sergeants in the

Figure 5–4 Me on rifle range, 1976. By the look on my face, someone took this picture the day the trainee accidentally fired her weapon. Photographer unknown.

center of the firing line. Each trainee stopped in front of the drill sergeant, coming from the left and right, and would yell, "No brass, no ammo, Drill Sergeant" to show that they had cleared their weapon. The drill sergeant would insert a rod into the barrel of the M16, while the muzzle faced downrange, and pushed the rod toward the butt of the rifle to make sure there was no ammo in the rifle. God help a trainee if a drill sergeant pushed out a live round, which happened sometimes.

By 5:00 PM, the Company boarded the cattle cars and headed to the Company. Once unloaded, the trainees went to the barracks, put their gear up, and returned for the supper meal formation. One trainee per platoon stayed behind to guard the M16s. I marched the platoon to the mess hall and moved them through the front door in single file to the chow line. Again I sat at the Drill Sergeant table, had supper, and talked to the other Drill Sergeants regarding the events of the day and our schedule for the next day. Sergeant First Class Lake seized the opportunity to ask if I wanted to teach a class on low-crawling to the Company. Everyone at the table laughed, and I had to laugh at that comment, too.

After finishing their meal, the trainees wandered back to the barracks in small groups and cleaned their weapons before turning them into the arms room. Next, they prepared their uniform and polished boots for the next day. That evening, I had a serious talk about range safety with the trainee who had discharged her weapon, including when to lock and load a round, fire at a target, and clear the weapon. I had her stay standing in front of my desk while I worked simulating clearing her M16 many, many times. I left the platoon around 7:30 PM to head home. The next day duplicated the one before.

One day, we gathered in the day room for a meeting that the Company Commander had scheduled. I entered the day room through the front door, a single-story, white wood-frame building, sitting between two white wood-frame barracks with two floors, and furnished with a pool table, ping-pong table, and two tables with four chairs each. The Company Commander, Captain Palmer, a tall, slender, attractive woman and a good officer, stood at the front of the room. I pulled a chair away from the table and sat in between two open windows at the rear of the room. Captain Palmer began talking to us about using less profanity with the trainees. Right at the moment she spoke those words, trainees outside the window started talking in loud voices. I turned in my chair and yelled out the window, "Goddamn it, trainees—shut the hell up so I can hear!"

I turned back to face Captain Palmer and said: "Go ahead, ma'am."

Captain Palmer smiled and said, "Thank you, Sergeant Haynie, for making my point." Once she said that, everyone in the room burst into laughter, including Captain Palmer. I took a couple of seconds to put it together and then laughed with them. At least I helped everyone understand the purpose of the meeting. She had a point concerning profanity, and I was the worst offender. I tried to clean it up after her talk.

The burn-out rate for drill sergeants appeared high—and it was the same for divorce. A drill sergeant had a two-year requirement to stay on status; some could extend their drill sergeant status for one year. Three years was the most time he could stay on drill sergeant duty. We received an extra $50 a month for being on drill sergeant duty.

OLD FRIENDS

I found my personal time outside of work during the 21/2 years at Fort Jackson inadequate because I worked so much and didn't have time for other activities. But to my good luck, the Army assigned Vaydon Jacobs and Jeff Weatherbee to Fort Jackson, and they attended the Drill Sergeant Academy. I enjoyed having them at Fort Jackson, but both of their marriages were failing, too. I can't say why their marriages failed, but I'm sure the demands of the Army played a part—maybe their spouses felt abandoned, too.

I had a Yamaha 650 motorcycle, and Jeff had a motorcycle, too, as did several other NCOs in our companies. There were 12 of us with motorcycles, and we spent an occasional Sunday riding together. We stopped for lunch somewhere along the way and talked. A good time was had by everyone. Sometimes the riders brought their wives with them. But I found getting together hard because of our different training schedules. After I left Fort Jackson, Jeff and Gloria divorced, and I never saw Jeff or Gloria again. Vaydon and Lynda divorced a year later but remarried, and we wouldn't see each other again until ten years later, at Fort Bliss.

I dated, but finding the time was difficult. One evening during a cycle break, I stopped at a local bar and grill to have dinner and a drink. While eating my steak, baked potato, and salad I observed a young woman at the end of the bar talking to friends. She was younger than me, good-looking, a blonde with green eyes; she had a contagious laugh. I knew she could tell I was watching her and listening to the conversation. After my meal, I went to the bar and ordered a drink, Jim Beam and Coke, and started a conversation with her. I learned her name was Carol. Twenty minutes later, she said it was time for her to leave. She accepted my offer of a ride home, and we continued to get to know each other during the 15-minute drive. Once we arrived at her home, I dropped her off and got her phone number. It was after this first meeting that Carol and I dated on a regular basis.

Mike Dankert, my best friend and brother from Vietnam, contacted me to tell me that he and his wife were planning a vacation to Charleston, South Carolina, and wanted to stop by and visit. In Vietnam, Mike and I had hit it off at once, and our relationship developed into a friendship. Lieutenant Baxter promoted him to Sergeant, and he accepted responsibility without question and grew into a good leader. Mike mentored and watched over the newer guys. I believe most of the squad looked up to him. He was serious but could loosen up, given the opportunity. I had never gotten as close to another person as I had Mike. We protected each other from harm.

I hadn't seen Mike for seven years, and we didn't talk often. We let life get in the way. Mike and his wife drove to Fort Jackson as scheduled, I met them at the main gate, and Mike followed me to my apartment. We embraced, telling each other how much we missed the other; seeing Mike again reminded me of the old days. Because of my recent divorce and job, I wasn't good company or a good host. They stayed only a day and then left, heading on their vacation route. I regret to this day that my behavior wasn't better. It would be another nine years before I saw Mike again. We let life get in the way of our friendship.

Tweed moved back to the barracks to save money, so I needed another roommate. Sergeant First Class Jim Griffin, a Senior Drill Sergeant at Bravo Company, and I rented a three-bedroom, two-bath house not far from post. The owner had converted the garage into a bar and TV room, and it was a perfect place to unwind. Jim and I were in different Companies, so our schedules didn't have us home much at the same time.

CO-ED BASIC TRAINING

In the summer of 1977, the Army tested co-ed basic training. The all-male 1st Brigade assimilated our all-female Battalion into the Brigade. The first test kept the male and female companies separate but in the same Battalion, with the same training schedule. Female trainees did everything a male trainee did, except for the physical training test; the APFT had different standards for female and male. During training, the female trainee did as well as the male trainee, and we didn't experience many difficulties. Fraternization between the female and male trainees occurred but without any serious problems.

My platoon had exceptional performance for this cycle, and they excelled at every training task. Captain Palmer entered my platoon into the Battalion drill-and-ceremony competition, the first time a female platoon competed in the competition. My platoon was the only female platoon competing, and we had a good opportunity to win. Two months of training prepared them for this competition.

The platoon appeared nervous on the day of the competition. I told them of their many accomplishments during training, their marching ability, along with teamwork; they could outmarch the male platoons any day. During the competition, the platoon flawlessly executed every command I gave. I didn't see one error. We took only third place, but I was proud of their performance and told them so. At the dinner meal, we were to be the last platoon to eat. I marched my platoon to the front of the line and gave the order for them to enter the mess hall single file ahead of the other platoons. The other drills gave me some halfhearted grief, but I told them the platoon deserved to eat first today.

Graduation day arrived, and I had the opportunity to talk with parents, siblings, grandparents, and spouses of the trainees in my platoon before and after graduation. Most parents told me that we, the Drill Sergeants, accomplished in nine weeks what they had tried to do in 18 or more years. The parents were proud of their child who left for basic training as a youngster and now was an adult—and, most importantly, a soldier. This made me proud, too. I could tell how proud the trainees were when they marched across the parade field the final time on Graduation Day. They were soldiers.

During the cycle break, I sat at the bar in my house having a Jim Beam and Coke, studying for the Drill Sergeant of the Cycle award. Captain Palmer recommended me for the competition with many other Drill Sergeants in the Battalion. The board had a mixture of senior NCOs who had drill-sergeant experience or were still on status. They evaluated my platoon statistics for marksmanship, APFT results, and end-of-cycle test results and asked technical and current-events questions.

After two hours of studying, I heard a collision at the intersection in front of the house. I ran out front and saw a car in the side yard, with two young adults, a male and a female, standing next to it. I asked if they were OK, and they replied "Yes." I looked at the intersection and saw a motorcycle lying on the ground with a body next to it. I ran to the body and noticed a young boy around 16 years old, wearing only cutoff blue jean shorts, not moving and lying in a pool of blood next to his bike. I searched his body for injuries and asked him questions to see if he would respond. Then I spotted the massive head wound. As I stood there for several seconds, I had flashes of the wounded or killed platoon brothers in Vietnam, but I turned them off so I could help the young man. I couldn't find a pulse and thought he'd died on impact. Neighbors circled around the wreck to see what had happened, so I went inside the house, got my bedspread, and covered the teenager's body. Several minutes after I'd covered his body, the paramedics and police arrived. The paramedics pulled the bedspread off to examine the teenager. One paramedic said he found a faint pulse and attempted CPR but within a minute pronounced him dead. It appeared I couldn't escape death.

The next morning at 8:00 AM, I reported to the Drill Sergeant of the Cycle board. The board members asked many questions, and I believe I gave good answers to their questions. They never told me if I missed a question or not. They read and questioned my training results, and I answered each, giving more information on how the platoon had achieved the results that they did. I must confess that, while meeting with the board, my mind kept going back to the young teenager who'd died the night before. I didn't think I did well. Later that day, Captain Palmer called me into her office and told me the board had selected me for the Drill Sergeant of the Cycle for the Battalion. It surprised me, but I was honored to receive the recognition. I thanked my assistant Drill Sergeant because it wouldn't have been possible without her hard work and dedication. The Drill Sergeant of the Cycle wore a braided blue rope around his drill sergeant hat for the next cycle to signify his achievement and received a letter of commendation from the Battalion Commander and Brigade Commander.

I felt sorry for the two kids whose car had killed the motorcyclist; they would live with this for the rest of their lives. I later learned that the police didn't bring charges against the driver of the car. They were not speeding, drinking, doing drugs, or driving recklessly. The teenager driving the motorcycle, with no working lights, had run a stop sign, and the driver didn't see him or have time to stop.

INTEGRATED BASIC TRAINING

Army Chief of Staff General Rogers approved consolidated basic training for men and women with a new program of instruction. Integrated training began at Fort Jackson, South Carolina, in October 1977. Basic-training Companies would have all-female and all-male platoons. The Army ended the Women's Army Corps in October 1978, and the Army assigned female soldiers to the branches of the Army instead of them being detailed. The Women's Army Corps no longer existed.

After the last training cycle, we went co-ed at the Company level. My Company Commander, Captain Palmer, volunteered me to work with the Chaplain during a cycle break to conduct seminars for drill sergeants and spouses on training female soldiers. I believe both the male drill sergeants and the spouses were apprehensive about training female soldiers. I thought of my first meeting with the Battalion Commander almost two years earlier and how my attitude about training females had changed. They are soldiers.

The female soldiers were on the top floor, and the male soldiers were on the bottom floor. Each floor had its own latrine, toilets, and showers, with a staircase to separate the two floors. I had only one co-ed basic training cycle, and I thought it went well. I didn't have problems in the platoon, and the men and women worked together when necessary and helped each other. I don't know what happened when I went home in the evenings.

When I had two months left on drill sergeant duty, Captain Palmer assigned me to the Arms Room because I didn't have enough time to be with a platoon for the training cycle. The Arms Room was in a single-story white framed building, sitting on a concrete pad, that provided a secure room for the Company weapons. The Company stored the M16s in a custom, vault-like room, where trainees would sign out their M16s in the morning and, at the end of a training day, turn the weapons in for accountability and secure them in the vault. I agreed with her decision because not being with a platoon of trainees would help me decompress before my next assignment.

WAYNE BECOMES A DRILL SERGEANT

One morning my replacement, Wayne, assigned by Battalion, reported to the Company commander, Captain Palmer. When Wayne came back from Germany, he went to Fort Leonard Wood, Missouri. He called me when he got orders to Fort Jackson, and I talked to Captain Palmer. She got him assigned to the Company. Being with Wayne again made my last couple of months easier, and, for a short period, the four of us were together again: Vaydon, Jeff, Wayne, and I. But under the circumstances—divorce, being a drill sergeant, and me scheduled to leave Fort Jackson, we didn't get together much.

Our hometown newspaper, *The Columbus Ledger*, wrote an article on Wayne and me. Wayne responded to the staff writer, Liz Benham, in a telephone interview June 29, 1978. The newspaper printed the photograph with the article.

When Glyn and John Haynie joined the Army in 1968, the Vietnam War was at its height. Being brothers, one of them could've been exempted from combat duty under military policy.

"But everyone was going," said John in a telephone conversation from Fort Jackson, South Carolina, where he's stationed. "We just felt it our duty to do our part."

He added the fact that his father, who lives with their mother in Waverly Hall, Georgia, and who was retired Army, didn't have much influence on their decision to serve. But joining the Army "was just something we always knew we would do."

"Our father didn't say anything about our going to Vietnam— being military oriented. But I'm sure, as a father, he really didn't want us to go at all. But he realizes being in the service is part of our obligation."

Recently Glyn handed over his drill sergeant hat to John, as the latter replaced him in Company E, 1st Battalion 1st Basic Training Brigade at Fort Jackson. The 28-year-old Glyn went on to Santa Ana, California.

But they've been stationed together often during their career, said John, who's a year older than his brother. "At Fort Benning, where we came into the service, at Fort Gordon, Georgia, Germany, and in Vietnam."

There was plenty of sibling rivalry when they were boys, said John. But that's changed over the years. "We're both professionals at our jobs, and now we really don't have any conflict about who's the best or things like that."

They prefer being stationed together, he continued. "We're very close, and it's nice to have family around when you're away from home."

They flew to Vietnam on the same airplane. "We were on the same set of orders but doing different jobs. Then he went to Germany a year before I did, and, while he was over there, I got orders and asked if it could be arranged for us to be together.

"There've been situations where one of us was the other's boss, but again there was no problem—we're both professionals."

And when he followed Glyn into drill sergeant school, the latter did give him some tips on what to expect, said John, adding sheepishly, "but I've got a little more temper than he has and bossed him around a bit when we were kids."

Figure 5–5 Left to Right: Me giving my Drill Sergeant Hat to my brother, Wayne Haynie, May 1978. Wayne was my replacement on Drill Sergeant Duty. Photographer unknown.

When I had four months left on drill sergeant status, I contacted the Department of Army Infantry Enlisted Branch to learn of my next assignment. The NCO in charge of assignments told me I'd go to Germany. I pled with him for a different assignment, stateside, and he said units in Germany needed my MOS. I wanted to return to an infantry unit, but my earlier experience convinced me not to go back to Germany, where I'd had such a terrible experience with soldiers using drugs and alcohol, and with racial intolerance.

Looking at my options, I could extend a year on drill sergeant duty. I was sure Captain Palmer would approve the extension, or I could volunteer for recruiting duty. These appeared to be my only options. Extending on drill sergeant duty might work, but it would be only a temporary fix. So going on recruiting duty became my only choice. The recruiting-duty selection process was similar to Drill Sergeant duty in that an NCO volunteered, or the Department of Army selected him.

Captain Palmer heard I wanted to volunteer for recruiting duty and called me into her office for an informal meeting. She was a good officer, and I respected some of the leadership traits she possessed, such as listening to subordinates and caring for the soldiers you worked with. I entered the office and took a seat in front of her desk, and she talked about me leaving the unit and appreciated my hard work during the last two years. Then she told me that going into recruiting duty would be a career-choice mistake. She came to Fort Jackson from being a Company Commander in recruiting before this assignment. She said recruiting was a thankless job and that meeting monthly recruiting objectives was difficult. Captain Palmer recommended that I reconsider my choice. I told her recruiting was my only choice, and she told me she had to at least try to talk me out of my decision. I left her office with some doubt regarding my choice, and this went against my rule to never volunteer.

VOLUNTEER FOR RECRUITING

I learned a recruiting team would arrive at Fort Jackson the next week to interview NCOs who had an interest in recruiting duty. I scheduled an appointment and showed up on time at the building where the recruiting team would be available for interviews. I approached a young sergeant at the desk, and he directed me to a Sergeant First Class sitting in a metal gray chair behind a long folding table covered in papers and brochures.

I walked up to his table, stopped in front of him, and said, "Good morning. I'm Sergeant Haynie, and I'm interested in learning about recruiting duty."

The Sergeant First Class looked up, with his blond hair falling over his eyes and ears, and replied, "Do you always wear your hat indoors?"

"Do you always wear your hair that long?" I snapped. Fort Jackson permitted wearing a drill sergeant hat indoors, and he should've known the rules before opening his mouth.

I finished the interview, and, several weeks later, I received notification that Recruiting Command had accepted me for recruiting duty. I went to the four weeks' recruiting school, Fort Benjamin Harrison at Indianapolis, Indiana, May 1978. The course was a salesman course, and the product the U.S. Army. The instructors taught the Lee Dubois sales techniques, "What to say, when to say it, and how to say it—what to ask, when to ask it, and how to ask it," and had us memorizing Army Enlistment Standards Regulations. The instructors emphasized closing the sale during each phase of the course. We learned how to keep the record of each prospect from the first interview through completing the enlistment paperwork. I was amazed at the amount of paperwork to complete for one recruit to enlist in the Army.

Being a salesman wasn't me, but I would learn to live with my decision. I didn't find the course difficult, and I graduated June 2, 1978. The recruiting station in Santa Ana, California, was my first recruiting assignment. I'd never lived on the west coast before this assignment. The Department of Army selected me for promotion and added me to the E7 list not long after I graduated.

Carol and I married, in a small ceremony, early June 1978, not long after I returned from Recruiting School. Soon after getting married, we packed a U-Haul trailer with my motorcycle and the rest of our belongings and attached the trailer to the car. We drove west on Interstate 20 for the 2,787-mile trip.

Being on Drill Sergeant duty was my most demanding assignment but the most rewarding, too. I looked forward to going to work each day and working with the professional NCOs and officers of my Company and teaching trainees. I found I loved teaching.

June 1978—I'm 28 years old, divorced and remarried, with three children (but this time the children weren't with me), and leaving for my sixth assignment in ten years.

CHAPTER 6

RECRUITING, SANTA ANA, CALIFORNIA

"Today's Army Wants to Join You"

—Army Slogan

The trip took five days of driving west, toward the coast; I'd never been to California. It shocked us how long it took to drive across Texas; it appeared we would never get through the state. When I pulled into the recruiting station in Santa Ana, California, we were hot, tired, and hungry. Carol and I found the office on the main road going through town and the parking lot behind the office, so we parked there. All services—Army, Marine, Navy, and Air Force—had an office in the same building. A year later, all services would move their offices to a shopping center five miles south of the current building.

REPORTING FOR WORK

The station commander, Staff Sergeant Don Cox, my height, balding, and with a pleasant smile, and the Assistant Area Commander (AAC), Sergeant First Class Lowery, greeted us upon our arrival. Sergeant First Class Lowery, a tall NCO with a medium build who had the air of a used-car salesman, introduced us to everyone in the office. After the introductions, he asked if we wanted to eat first or look at some apartments he had ready to show us. We said we were hungry and went across the street to a Mexican restaurant for an early dinner. I don't remember eating much Mexican food before, so this was another new experience. I had beef enchiladas, nothing too adventurous. It was an enjoyable meal, and I developed a taste for Mexican food while living in California.

After the meal, Sergeant First Class Lowery took us apartment hunting. On the first stop, we rented a one-bedroom apartment in Tustin, around 15 minutes from the office, depending on how heavy the traffic was. The traffic in Southern California was terrible. I'd never seen so many cars at one time on the road. The apartments were newer, one-story, with a swimming pool and Jacuzzi hot tub. Southern California had a high cost of living standard, and the only extra money we received was the $50 a month recruiter pay, the same as my drill sergeant pay. It would be hard to make it on the salary of a Staff Sergeant.

When I reported, the unit organization differed from any assignment I had before recruiting duty. At the lowest level was a Recruiting Station (a sales office), which reported to an Area Commander (Captain) and an Assistant Area Commander (Master Sergeant). The Area was composed of many Stations, and an Area reported to a District Commander (Lieutenant Colonel) and a District Sergeant Major. The District had many Areas and reported to a Region Commander (Colonel) and a Region Command Sergeant Major. The Region Commander reported to the United States Army Recruiting Command (USAREC) Commander, a Major General. There were five recruiting Regions in the United States. I found the recruiting chain of command confusing, unlike any earlier army-unit assignment.

Recruiting Command changed the unit configuration several years after I arrived. A Region became a Brigade with a Brigade Commander and Command Sergeant Major. A District became a Battalion with a Battalion Commander and Battalion Sergeant Major. An Area became a Company with a Company Commander and First Sergeant. The Station remained the same, with a station commander and recruiters. This appeared more like the earlier assignments I'd had before arriving at recruiting. All recruiters are Noncommissioned Officers, Sergeant, Staff Sergeant, and Sergeant First Class.

MY NEW DUTIES

I must admit that I got off to a rocky start; I needed to transition from being a drill sergeant to a recruiter. When prospects walked into the office, they avoided my desk and looked for another recruiter who did not appear busy. It took a short while to figure out that I came to work each morning wearing my drill sergeant face and used my drill sergeant voice when talking to prospects. I had to learn to smile and talk nicely. And that is what I did!

My duties as a recruiter included going to my assigned high schools and talking to counselors and students about the Army. Several schools wouldn't allow recruiters on campus. The civilian community still had an unfavorable opinion of the Army because of the Vietnam War. I replaced any advertisement brochures that were outdated or low in stock. Along with the assignment of high schools, I had a list of names, phone numbers, and addresses of each junior and senior class where I made "cold" phone calls each day. The requirement was to make a defined number of phone calls, appointments, interviews, and enlistments each month. If I didn't make these requirements, I had everyone in the chain of command talking to me about what a "poor" soldier I was.

At times we paired up and canvassed areas where young people congregated. As strange as it sounds, we went to the bus station, Salvation Army, homeless shelters, and locations where homeless people hung out. Many young men and women came to southern California to make it rich in the entertainment industry or find a better-paying job that wasn't available in their hometown. Often, it wasn't long before they found themselves sleeping on the streets, and an offer to join the Army sounded enticing and like a way to improve their life. Most were highly qualified for the Army but had made a poor choice to come to southern California without much savings.

Making the recruiting mission quota each month became paramount to everything else. The USAREC Commander assigned the yearly mission during the recruiting year, July 1st through June 30th. The hours worked were long, and we worked most Saturdays and an occasional Sunday. If I made mission, and my station didn't, the command expected me to overachieve to make up any shortfall within the Station, Company, or Battalion. So I worked alongside the recruiters who were still working to make mission, normally late at night and on weekends. Ordering successful recruiters to make up enlistments for unsuccessful recruiters' quotas didn't result in the atmosphere of teamwork that the command had led us to believe it would. I assumed that commanders in recruiting thought that NCOs were not too bright.

The mission changed each month; it could be two enlistees or four enlistees a month. This may not sound like many people joining the Army in a given month, but finding qualified applicants could be difficult. It appeared the ones who wanted to join the Army failed the entrance examination or the physical examination, which led to more frustrations for the job.

Later on, during my recruiting career, the command assigned the mission by male and female, mental category from the entrance examination score, and whether or not the candidate had a high school diploma. This made it even more difficult to make my monthly mission. For example, and to keep it simple, I'd receive a mission for July for one male high school graduate with a test category of 3A (the highest), and I enlisted one male with a test category of 3B (next to the highest). I still wouldn't make mission because the one male wasn't a test category 3A, even though I enlisted one male. The command thought me a low-performing soldier for not making my recruiting goals and told me to work extra hours to make up the shortfall of the male 3A high school graduate. It appeared I was in a no-win situation every month.

Enlisting an applicant into the Army was a long process that took days, weeks, or months. Once I made an appointment, and the applicant showed, I conducted an interview, known as a "sales presentation." During the interview, I tried to discern their interest in the Army and what motivated them to join the Army and handle any objections they may have regarding joining the Army. Handling objections guided the applicant in telling me the real reason he'd said "No" to joining the Army, an important part of the interview. I wanted the applicant saying "Yes" to joining the Army at the end of the interview.

During the interview, I completed a Prospect Card. All forms used were Department of Army or Department of Defense forms. Intentionally entering false information on any form would be a serious offense, for which I could receive an Article 15 or court martial. I asked the applicant about their health history and any criminal record, including minor offenses, even traffic violations. If they admitted to a health condition or criminal offense that disqualified them from joining the Army, I ended the interview. Many applicants' health or criminal record disqualified them from joining. I could submit a waiver of exception for some health conditions and criminal offenses, and I needed to do extra paperwork and get approval from the Chain of Command.

After the first interview, the applicant took a practice Armed Services Vocational Aptitude Battery (ASVAB) test. The ASVAB is a timed multi-aptitude test. The practice test gives a good indication of how well the applicant would do on the actual ASVAB and gave indications of job skills the applicant had that would help him qualify for the Army. After the practice test, I'd take their height and weight. It amazed me the number of people who wanted to join the Army but couldn't because they didn't meet the weight standards.

Once the applicant agreed to join the Army, I had them take the actual ASVAB and then complete the enlistment packet. The enlistment paperwork, a multiform and multi-page document, needed the information entered to be correct and legible. The applicant and I both signed the form stating the information entered was true and correct. I then scheduled a date for the physical and enlistment in the Army. I picked the applicant up early on the morning of enlistment and drove them to the Military Entrance and Process Station (MEPS) in Los Angeles. Then I drove them home after they enlisted. Departing for LA at 5:30 AM, the drive took about one hour, and the drive home, at 5:00 PM, took more than three hours, caught in stop-and-go traffic all the way to the recruiting station.

I never knew what specific jobs were available. The recruiting policy stated not to talk jobs to an applicant. That is great in theory, but seldom could I convince an applicant to go through the enlistment process without talking jobs. The guidance counselor at the MEPS had access to job openings and knew what the Army needed. They sold a job to the applicant based on the needs of the Army.

An applicant, as a rule, enlisted into the Delayed Entry Program (DEP) because a school start date would be weeks, months, or even a year away from the job for which they enlisted, and they seldom went active duty on the day of enlistment. I followed up with the enlistees during the DEP time to keep their interest in the Army and job choice. I kept them motivated about going active duty in the Army, all the while looking for new applicants.

I have to admit that I found recruiting not the most exciting job I've had in the Army, and I missed being with troops. However, I found the job rewarding when helping a young person, providing direction and improving their life—an opportunity they may not have received other-wise—by joining the Army. It was always a special day when an enlistee returned home from training a new person, a soldier. Recruiting provided the opportunity to work with many excellent NCOs and officers, too.

FIRST YEAR

I was doing well my first year as a recruiter and on track to win the award of Rookie Recruiter of the Year for my Battalion, as I exceeded my enlistment objectives so far. On February 1, 1979, the Army promoted me to Sergeant First Class (E7). My promotion coincided with the station commander, Staff Sergeant Cox, leaving for another assignment in recruiting. The Company commander assigned me as the Station Commander. In a large station like ours, six recruiters, the Station Commander wasn't assigned an individual mission; he managed the entire recruiter's combined mission. But I remained on a mission until the end of the year.

Recruiting Command loved giving end-of-year awards, and each Battalion made receiving an award a production. We dressed in dress blue uniforms and attended a banquet for the awards. I always thought it a little overboard but followed along with the program. At the end of my first year, I won the Rookie Recruiter of the Year award, and our Station took the Top Recruiting Station award, too. The recruiters and I were proud of our achievements. We went to work the next day and started a new year. The motto for recruiters was "A hero today and a zero tomorrow." The command didn't care about our past achievements.

Figure 6–1 Me receiving the Battalion Rookie Recruiter of the Year Award, July 1979. I believe the officer is Major General William L. Mundie, the USAREC Commander. Photographer unknown.

I continued to run and work out with different recruiters, but Staff Sergeant Jim Wold became my main workout partner, a recruiter, and friend in the Station. Jim was shorter than me, had a great sense of humor, and looked like the actor Peter Sellers. Not too far from the office, we found a running obstacle course at a park, and we went several times a week. Jim's wife, Barbara, and Carol became fast friends, too. We spent weekends together going to the beach for boogie boarding and Big Bear for snow skiing. The first year skiing, I wasn't a good student. In general, I picked up sports with no problems, but skiing was different. After several runs downhill and falling many times, I thought I was getting better. While waiting in line for the lift, the man behind me asked, "Did you leave any snow on the mountain?" Everyone in line laughed, and I looked at my snowsuit and found it covered in snow after my many falls. Although embarrassed, I had to laugh, too.

THE SOFTBALL TEAM

Jim and I started up an Army Recruiting slow-pitch softball team. We could play softball year round in southern California. The softball team was an excellent source of advertisement in the community. Battalion even furnished the uniforms and hats. The softball uniforms were white with blue trim, with "Army" written across the front, worn with blue socks and hat that had "Army" in white embroidery across the front. At every game, we had young people and parents approach us and ask about the Army. I don't know if we actually got any enlistments—there was no data available—but we got noticed. The local newspaper carried a short article about the team both years, not because we were Army but for our ranking in the league.

We got Army recruiters within our Company to take part. We were short one player, so I approached the Marine Corps recruiting Station Commander, a tall, muscular black NCO, and he looked like a Marine. I asked him if he would play on our team. To my surprise, the Gunny agreed. He wore the Army baseball uniform and hat with pride. *Semper Fi!*

I recall one evening we had a playoff game for the city championship for our division. The score was close, 3–2, and we were losing, but we were playing the best defensive game the team had ever played. I approached the plate to bat in the last inning with one out, and I hit a single up the middle. The Gunny, batting left-handed, batted next and plowed a line drive along the first-base line. The base coach told me to stay until he made sure the right fielder couldn't catch the ball and then sent me off running as the ball went past the right fielder. I rounded second base and continued to third base, all the while hearing the gunny not far behind me. The third-base coach waved me around, and I headed for home plate. I saw the ball coming toward home plate as I slid into home and then guided my right foot into the catcher's mitt; the ball hit my foot and bounced out as I slid across home plate. Before I could stand, Gunny slid headfirst across home plate. While still lying on the ground, he jumped on top of me, hugging me hard. We thought we'd won the World Series. We won the game 4–3 and went on to the city championship game. We won the city championship game, too. Both years our team went to the city finals for our category.

David and John flew to our home in Santa Ana in the summer of 1979. Paula decided that Brooke was too young to fly. I can't explain how excited I was when I picked them up at the Los Angeles airport. On the hour drive home, we talked about the activities we would do and the places we would go during their visit. They stayed for the summer, attended my softball games, and helped out by being batboys for the team.

We visited Disneyland on one Saturday. The boys enjoyed the rides, but my favorite memory is Space Mountain. Carol didn't go on the ride, so it was the three of us. John, being the youngest, five years old, sat with me, which meant David, eight years old, had to sit alone in the car in front of me. David wasn't happy about riding alone but said he would do it. During the entire ride, I watched David, and he kept his eyes closed during most of the ride. When the ride ended and we got off on the platform, he let me know he wasn't happy having to go on the ride alone. David said John was my favorite because he had to sit alone on the ride. The following weekend, we went to another amusement park, Knotts Berry Farm, for a day of fun. Several evenings after work, we went to the beach to swim and boogie board. The summer ended as fast as it had started, and it was time for David and John to return to their mothers. That was a sad day.

IRANIAN CRISIS

On November 4, 1979, Iranian students stormed the U.S. Embassy and took fifty-two American diplomats and citizens as hostages. They held them until January 20, 1981. Much debate occurred in the United States on what action we should take. The hostage crisis caused the media to investigate if a rise in patriotism and enlistments resulted.

The NBC television station in Los Angeles came to Santa Ana and interviewed me for the nightly news coverage concerning increased enlistments into the Army because of the crisis. The Battalion advertisement representative, a civilian from N. W. Ayer, called and advised me on what not to say: "Don't compare this crisis to Vietnam, and don't mention Vietnam" were my instructions. But I ignored this advice because it let me talk about my disappointment after coming home from Vietnam.

Patt Morrison interviewed me, with other recruiters, for the *Los Angeles Times Orange County News* on December 11, 1979. This is part of the interview, as written by Patt Morrison.

RECRUITERS FIND THEY'RE GETTING CALLS

They're not yet standing in line for dog tags, but some Orange County young men have been letting military recruiters know they're "mad as hell" about what's going on in Iran, and would enlist at the first gunshot.

"They're not exactly knocking the doors down, but (recruitment) this November is better than last November," said a Marine Corps major.

Whether the fervor has resulted in any enlistments is difficult to say. "We just don't ask a kid if he's joining because he's mad at Iran," the officer said.

But a patriotic resurgence is showing up among some youths who, 10 years ago, might have been burning draft cards instead of calling up their local recruiters.

Whether or not the Iranian crisis is responsible for the increase in volunteers, the evidence of renewed interest in and respect for the military has buoyed the spirits of many recruiters.

"It's a refreshing attitude," said Sgt. Glyn Haynie, an Army recruiting officer in Santa Ana. "Normally, the attitude toward the military has not been very favorable since the Vietnam War. It's nice that people care about their country again."

Haynie said he couldn't say whether there have been any enlistments because of the situation in Iran but "some (callers) indicate if we did (get involved), they'd be glad to go. . . ."

The Iranian crisis went into the old-news cycle as fast as it made the news. I don't remember enlistments increasing during this period, but I saw a change in how people talked to us and treated us. They appeared to have a more favorable opinion of the Army. A year or two before I came into recruiting, recruiters wore civilian clothes when going to high schools and other events. They had to hide the fact that they were proud soldiers. The American people still treated the American soldier as if he, the soldier, had invaded Vietnam and the war had been his fault.

The Army created Delta Force because of the growing threat of terrorism around the world, and it became certified as mission capable in the fall of 1979, right before the Iran hostage crisis. I believe it was in early January 1980 that I received a letter from the Department of Army requesting I try out for the new unit. A good number of infantry NCOs received the same letter, so it wasn't a unique request for me to try out. I considered taking the Army up on its offer but decided to stay in recruiting after I learned of the requirements for becoming a member of

Delta Force: accepting assignment to an airborne unit was one of them, and more than a year of training was necessary.

A BABY AND A MOVE

One year to the day after the beginning of the Iran Hostage Crisis—November 4, 1980—Carol and I had our first son, my third son, Nathan, born in Orange, California. The doctors predicted his due date three weeks earlier, so we had some concern. They were wrong. Nathan was healthy, and the delivery went smoothly. I went to the delivery room to see his birth, but I was told to stand near the head of the bed.

In early December 1980, Carol, Nathan, and I left California for my new assignment at State College, Pennsylvania. Four months earlier, I'd requested a transfer to leave California, because of the cost of living and to get closer to David, John, and Brooke. State College was the only Station Commander position available.

December 1980—I'm 30 years old, married, with a new son, my fourth child, seventh assignment in 12 years and five months.

RECRUITING, STATE COLLEGE, PENNSYLVANIA

"Be All You Can Be"

—ARMY SLOGAN

W e arrived at State College early January 1981 after visiting family and David, John, and Brooke during December. I saw State College as a quaint college town—Penn State—and found the residents clannish to outsiders—in particular, if you didn't work at the university. Recruiting in State College differed from California because occasionally we had protesters milling around the entrance to our office. We would enter the office through the back door and telephone scheduled appointments to use the back door. I asked why they were protesting, and the reply was "the Army." I believe they protested because that was what college students did. The recruiters were great NCOs, and we continued to enlist our quota each month.

The first summer at State College, David, John, and Brooke came up to spend the summer. We lived in Lemont, and our house stood at the base of Mount Nittany. I took David and John hiking along the trails from our house into the mountains on weekends. We scheduled a hiking trip with a neighbor and his son on a Sunday afternoon. But John, at seven years old, left the house, telling no one, and went up the trail alone. I didn't realize he'd left without David and me for more than an hour.

The neighbor and I hiked up the mountain yelling John's name and searching the terrain but couldn't find him. When we got back to the house, I called the police. The police dispatched search teams and a helicopter to find him. It impressed me with the way the police and search parties responded so fast to my request for help. The helicopter flew over the mountain trails calling his name through a loudspeaker. When it got too dark, they called off the search. Early the next morning, around 1:00 AM, the state prison, almost five miles from the house, called me and said that two prison guards on patrol had found John and had him at the prison. I thought of leaving him there, but I drove to the prison to pick him up and bring him home. When I saw him, I didn't know if I'd hug him or ground him for life. I chose the hug. This episode scared me.

The next morning, I questioned John about his night on the mountain. He needed to understand how serious his actions were. John said he wanted to surprise me and went up the trail early but got bored and headed up the mountain. He said it didn't take long for him to get lost, and, when dark came, he covered up in leaves to keep warm. And that is where the two prison guards found him, put him in their vehicle, and drove him to the prison. I knew he hadn't done this on purpose, but I grounded him to remind him that he couldn't go off by himself.

My assignment at State College lasted two years, and then the Battalion assigned me as the Battalion Assistant Operations NCO (S3). I reported to the Operations NCO, in New Cumberland Army Depot, New Cumberland. The Battalion headquarters was on the depot. The depot, originally built in 1918, was located across the river, several miles from downtown Harrisburg. Once I received orders, we packed up and moved for my new assignment.

We purchased a townhouse in Etters, around 15 minutes from the Battalion headquarters. David, at 12 years old, came to live with us not long after we moved into our house. On February 1, 1983, the Army promoted me to Master Sergeant (E8), and on February 13, 1983, Carol gave birth to Bryan.

Carol went into labor during a major snowstorm, so David and I kept shoveling the snow out of the driveway. As soon as we cleared the driveway, the snowplow operator would push the snow back into the driveway, or it would snow some more. We got it cleared enough to get the car out. Over the last two days, we'd received 24 inches of snow. Luckily, the state had one lane open on the Interstate, so we could drive the 15 miles to the hospital.

The doctor delivered Bryan within hours of our checking into the hospital. I stayed in the delivery room to see his birth. I asked the doctor if I could stand where he stood so I could watch the delivery. The doctor said, "Sure. I can use all the help I can get." Thank goodness, he didn't ask me for any help. It was an amazing experience to watch the actual birth of my child!

It wasn't long after my assignment as the assistant operations NCO that the operations NCO made Sergeant Major and left the Battalion, leaving me to fill his vacant position. I found being in charge of the daily operations of the Battalion recruiting mission challenging and fun. I became proficient at the job and instituted new tracking methods for enlistments and helped counselors at the MEPS close hard sales. I worked well with the Battalion Company Commanders and First Sergeants.

Each quarter the Battalion Commander and Sergeant Major had the Station Commanders, First Sergeants, Company Commanders, and Battalion staff attend training. This quarter, the training was at a hotel in Lancaster. The training introduced any new information about recruiting and always covered not making mission. I found it boring because it was always the same speech. At the noon break for lunch, the group of forty officers and NCOs walked to the hotel restaurant for lunch. I noticed many of my fellow NCOs talking and pointing to a table in the center of the restaurant. I looked in the direction they were pointing, and, to my amazement, I saw Bob Hope eating lunch with one other person at his table. When he saw us, he stopped eating and motioned for us to come over to his table. Here sat a man who was a superstar, and he stops eating to acknowledge a group of soldiers. One by one, he said hello and shook each person's hand. As I shook his hand, I remembered the last time I'd seen Mr. Hope, in Chu Lai, Vietnam, when he was on his 1969 USO tour. I sat a good distance from the stage, and here I was today, shaking his hand.

On the way back to the meeting room, we made sure we didn't disturb Mr. Hope as he finished his lunch. Once seated, the training started, and after 15 minutes, I thought it would be a good idea to take a nap. Before I closed my eyes, the door to the room opened, and in walked Mr. Hope. He smiled and looked embarrassed as everyone in the room stood and applauded.

He apologized for interrupting our meeting and asked the Battalion Commander if he could practice his monologue one last time before going to the Lancaster County Fair. Mr. Hope spent more than an hour telling his jokes, with everyone laughing the whole time, and he talked with us. I must confess that he was funnier in person, and you could tell that he wanted to be around soldiers and respected them. I thought how unbelievable it was that a person as famous as Bob Hope would stop and spend time with us. What an honor!

FIRST SERGEANT ASSIGNMENT

I longed for the day I'd become a First Sergeant. In early August 1983, the Battalion Commander called me into his office and said the Harrisburg Company First Sergeant had retired and that I was the new First Sergeant. The news of my new job and being a First Sergeant excited me. I thought it might have been more rewarding if I'd become a First Sergeant in an Infantry Company, but those days were long gone. The First Sergeant I replaced had an earlier assignment as a recruiter in the Station I enlisted from in Columbus, Georgia. It took several months to get my feet on the ground, but I worked with outstanding NCOs, which made the job easier, and I looked forward to going to work every day.

On the morning of October 25, 1983, we received notification of American forces armed invasion of the island of Grenada, code-named Operation Urgent Fury. President Reagan sent a force of 7,600 troops, composed of Ranger Battalions, 82nd Airborne Division, Marines, Delta Force, and Navy SEALS. The People's Revolutionary Government had taken over the government, and President Reagan's primary concern was the 600 medical students on the island.

The American forces fought 1,500 Grenadian soldiers and 700 armed Cuban nationals. Most were manning defensive positions. The invasion lasted a week before the American forces defeated the ruling military force, and a Democratic government replaced the Revolutionary Military Council. We as recruiters saw a brief upsurge of interest in joining the Army, but the interest died as fast as it started. I found it amazing that the interest in the Army by young men and women increased whenever a military action occurred.

Within seven months of my becoming the First Sergeant, the Battalion Commander relieved the Company Commander. The Battalion Commander called me into his office next and told me to take charge of the Company; he added that he had complete confidence in my ability. He stated that he didn't know when a replacement Company Commander would arrive. This left me in charge of the Company without an officer to help lead. Not having an officer assigned left me no way to share the workload. I remained in charge of the Harrisburg Company for five months before a replacement Company Commander arrived. This put more strain on an already-strained marriage. I stayed on the road visiting one or more of the six recruiting Stations in the Company on any given day, getting home late and sometimes staying overnight at a Station. The recruiting Stations were in Harrisburg, Lancaster, Lebanon, Elizabethtown, Reading, and Temple.

DAD IS DYING

In the middle of July 1984, I received a phone call from Wayne telling me dad was getting worse and that I should come home and see him before he dies. I went to the Battalion Sergeant Major to ask for ten days of leave to see my dying father. The Sergeant Major approved the leave but asked if I could do the visit in less than ten days or, even better, wait until the Company makes mission. I told him I needed ten days now and would combine the leave with the time I would take off for the summer. I couldn't believe he'd even consider asking a question like that. I gathered Carol, Nathan, and Bryan and drove the 800 miles to Waverly Hall, Georgia, where my parents lived. David didn't go because he visited his mom during the summer and was already with her. Wayne and Dee were at mom's house, waiting for me.

We visited dad every day at the nursing home. On my last day, I went to see dad, and he was lying in bed in his room. He saw me enter the room and motioned for me to come closer.

I sat on the edge of the bed and asked, "Dad, what do you need?"

In a low voice, he asked, "When are you leaving?"

"Tomorrow morning," I replied.

He looked me in the eye and said, "I love you."

"I love you, too," I replied with tears in my eyes. And then we hugged. Something we never did.

This is the first time I ever remember my father using those three words, "I love you." It stunned me, but I soon realized he knew his time was ending. I left the nursing home and went back to my mother's house. The next morning, with the car packed, we headed to Atlanta. Carol, Nathan, and Bryan were taking a flight out of Atlanta to her parents' home in Portland, Oregon.

Once at the airport, I got them on the flight, walked back to the car, and headed to Pennsylvania. Carol and I had decided that our six-year marriage was over before the trip to see my dad, and I knew this was goodbye when she boarded the plane. Again, it was several factors that ended the marriage, and, out of respect, I won't discuss them here. But one of the primary reasons was me not being home enough. Taking the First Sergeant position was the breaking point for Carol. I traveled several days during the week and worked 10 to 12 hours a day and many weekends. I believe she'd just had enough. This was the second time I allowed my job to take priority. But I decided I didn't want to be away from my children.

Carol went back to college and had a job, so we decided Nathan should live with me, and he returned in August. David, still living with me, returned from visiting his mother in August. Bryan would come home to live with me in March because of Carol's schedule. We decided it was best that Nathan and Bryan stay with me. I and my three sons, David, Nathan, and Bryan, made a new life for ourselves. Over the Labor Day weekend, I got a new Company Commander, which would help by cutting my time at work, making it easier to spend time with the boys. During this time, David turned 13 years old and was a big help around the house and with Nathan and Bryan. I couldn't have managed to be a single dad without him.

During the early morning of September 9, 1984, Wayne called and told me Dad had died and that I should come home. After the phone call, I drove to Battalion Headquarters, went to the Sergeant Major's office, and told him I needed emergency leave because my father had died.

He responded, "You just saw your father. Why do you need to go again?"

"To attend the funeral and help my mother," I replied with anger in my voice.

The Sergeant Major looked me in the eye and said: "He's dead, and there's nothing you can do for your father by taking leave." Before I could reply, he asked, "So why go?"

"That's bullshit, Sergeant Major. Sign my leave, or I'll get the Battalion Commander to sign it," I replied with more anger.

The Sergeant Major signed my leave for five days. Our relationship would never be the same again, and it got worse after I returned from leave. The day my father died, Carol flew back to Pennsylvania to get her belongings and car. I asked her to watch the boys while I went to Georgia, and she agreed. I got a flight that afternoon to Atlanta, and Wayne picked me up for the hour drive home. When we got back to

Columbus, we headed straight to a bar for drinks and to talk about getting things ready for the funeral.

Dad had a military funeral at Fort Benning, and Wayne and I wore our Dress Green uniform. I became emotional when I heard the three-volley salute, which represents duty, honor, and country, and then a solo bugler played "Taps" without accompaniment. Tears clouded my eyes while the notes of the bugler echoed throughout the cemetery; it was a sad day. I wanted the funeral to end so I could get away from the sadness. Not long after the final note played, we loaded into our cars and drove back to mom's house. I helped mom and Wayne get tasks done they needed help with, and the Army assigned a Casualty Assistance Officer to help my mother through the Veterans Administration (VA) survivor process. I flew back to Pennsylvania several days after the funeral.

David and I helped Carol pack her car and U-Haul trailer for her trip back to Oregon. I returned to work and had a new Company Commander to train. Officers had no practical experience in recruiting, which, I believed, made it harder for them. They attended a recruiting course before reporting to the Company. Being officers, they didn't need to do actual recruiting but only enforce the standards and do public speaking sometimes. Command held them accountable for the Company mission the same as the First Sergeant and everyone else—maybe even more than everyone else. Recruiting could ruin a career in months. The new Company Commander proved to be an effective leader. The leadership traits that this officer exhibited were character, integrity, and personal courage. It was easy to forget about these traits while in recruiting, and I appreciated the reminder.

In January 1985, the Sergeant Major asked if I'd go back and assume the duties of the Battalion Operations NCO, and I told him I wanted to stay with the Harrisburg Company as the First Sergeant. For two weeks, he didn't mention it. Then, one morning, the Sergeant Major showed up at the Company headquarters, which he seldom did, and as he walked through the front door, he said we needed to talk. I got up from my desk and greeted him. We walked to the coffee machine, and each filled a cup with fresh coffee. Then he pulled a chair up next to my desk. I assumed he wanted to talk concerning our recruiting mission; we weren't doing well this month meeting our quota.

He took a sip of coffee and said, "Haynie, I want you back at Battalion in Operations."

"Sergeant Major, I really enjoy being a First Sergeant and want to stay here," I replied, knowing this wasn't what he wanted to hear.

The Sergeant Major looked at me with a wry smile and said, "You are a single parent now." He paused for effect, took another sip of coffee, and continued, "How about I get you assigned to an Infantry unit in Korea?"

I looked at him with disbelief as he continued. "Who will take care of your children?"

"What the hell, Sergeant Major—is that a threat?" I choked out the words in a low voice.

He said, "Not a threat, Haynie, but I'll make it happen if you don't agree to come back to operations!"

I sat there red in the face, holding back the anger that was boiling to the surface, ready to erupt. The conversation ended. He stood, set his cup on the desk, and, without another word, he left the office. I sat there, unable to stand, for another ten minutes, staring out the office window digesting the conversation I'd had minutes earlier. I don't know why the Sergeant Major thought he had to threaten me; he was the Sergeant Major, and all he needed to do was tell me to report to Battalion.

I took the job at Battalion and reported within two weeks of our conversation. His office door angled across the hall from my desk, and I had to see him every day. I couldn't let my pride risk me being separated from my sons. This is how recruiting command operated—numbers are the only thing that matter, regardless of the leadership or the lack of leadership. The leadership trait that I learned from the Battalion Sergeant Major was to lead the opposite of how he led.

Several good things came out of the move to Battalion. I spent more time with the boys, and Nathan and Bryan spent less time in daycare. I exercised more, too. Every day at lunch, taking a 1½-hour lunch, I went to the gym to lift weights and then play in pickup basketball games. I ran on the days I didn't lift weights. I arrived at work around 7:00 AM and left at 6:30 PM, so the extra half-hour at lunch was insignificant. I met Sherrie during this time, an eye-catching woman, with sparkling green eyes, shoulder-length, light-brown hair, with a zest for life and intelligence—what a combination! On our third meeting, I asked her out on a date, and she met me at a club downtown in Harrisburg. We had drinks and talked the night away. When we left the club, we walked along the river facing the cool breeze and talked for another 30 minutes. We dated on a regular basis after this first date. As soon as I introduced her to the boys, she fell in love with them.

MIKE AND A REUNION

In the spring of 1985, I got a call regarding a Hill 4–11 Association having a reunion, their second. This was the first time I'd heard of the Association or reunions. Hill 4–11 was the firebase that our Company built in July-August 1969. The Battalion Commander named the firebase to display the joint effort of the 4th Army of the Republic of Vietnam (ARVN) Regiment and the 11th Infantry Brigade, hence the name "Hill 4–11." The Association included all units—infantry, cavalry, artillery, and engineers—who served on the firebase from 1969 until the Army abandoned it. A small group of infantry soldiers who'd served on the firebase in 1971 started the Association.

There were a number of reasons to have a reunion. Veterans who served together in the same unit or combat area have a bond, and this bond helped the veteran to survive the worst of times. It allows the veteran to reconnect and share his experiences, re-forge the brotherhood, and rekindle past friendships. A reunion can be therapeutic for some veterans as they renew the relationships of the past. For me, it's not the war stories or photographs but reconnecting with my brothers of First Platoon that was most important.

I contacted Mike, and we agreed to meet at the reunion, July 20–21, 1985, in St. Louis, Missouri. I hadn't seen Mike since 1976, when he

Figure 7-1 Left to Right—Me and Mike Dankert at the Hill 4-11 reunion St. Louis, Missouri, 1985. Photographer unknown.

visited me at Fort Jackson. David went to visit his mother for the summer. I flew to Oregon with Nathan and Bryan and left them so they could spend the rest of the summer with their mother. On the way back home, I stopped in St. Louis to attend the reunion. Seeing Mike, Dusty, and Chuck again made my day. Cliff Sivadge attended the reunion, too, and I spent time talking with him.

In Vietnam, I'd learned

Figure 7-2 Left to Right—Dusty Rhoades and Mike Dankert at the Hill 4-11 reunion having a serious talk. St. Louis, Missouri, 1985. Photographer unknown.

Dusty hailed from the western plains of Nebraska, where he was a deadly shot against prairie dogs and jackrabbits on his father's ranch.

Dusty was quiet but friendly and had the respect and trust of the platoon members of First Platoon. On July 14, 1969, he received life-threatening wounds while protecting his position on Hill 4–11. It was a tremendous relief for us all to see that he'd healed from his wounds and was doing well.

Figure 7–3 Left to Right—Me and Cliff Sivadge at the Hill 4–11 reunion St. Louis, Missouri, 1985. Photographer unknown.

Cliff Sivadge was a replacement after the casualties we suffered in August 1969, and he stood out among the replacements. He arrived in Vietnam early to mid-September and was from Iowa. While in Vietnam, Cliff was easygoing but serious if needed. He didn't act like someone who didn't need training; he wanted to learn. He was pleasant and quick to join a conversation. It was at the reunion that I learned that Cliff was at Fort Benning the same time I was. What a disappointment that neither of us knew the other was there.

I missed the next four reunions before I started attending most of them. I was still letting life get in the way. After the missed reunions, I

Figure 7–4 Left to right—Me, Chuck Council, Dusty Rhoades, and Mike Dankert at Hill 4–11 Reunion. July 20, 1990, Nashville, Tennessee. This is 5 years later but is the only photograph of the four of us. The photograph was taken by Sherrie Haynie.

did a better job of staying in touch. It wasn't until I retired at Fort Bliss, Texas, that I went to the next one, in 1990.

In the spring of 1986, I sold the townhouse, and we moved into an apartment to help reduce living expenses. The only negative was that David had to change schools. Not long after we moved, Mike called. He said he was going on a family vacation and driving through Pennsylvania and asked if he could visit for two days. Of course, I said, "Yes." I believe they arrived on a Friday afternoon and checked into a hotel near the apartment. The first night we had dinner at the apartment, and Mike and I sat around drinking Jim Beam and Coke and talking about our lives and the fun days in Vietnam.

On Saturday we went to the Vietnam War Memorial in Washington, D.C. which was only a three-hour drive from the apartment. I had my doubts about the Memorial, thinking a plain black granite wall below the ground surface showed disdain for the soldiers who'd fought the war and even the surviving Vietnam Veterans. When Mike and I approached

The Wall the first time, my opinion changed. Goosebumps appeared on my body, transmitting a tingling sensation all over. What I felt was hard to put into words: "inspired," "humble," "sad," "relieved," and "thankful" come to mind. I thought the Memorial a tribute honoring the men and women who'd fought and died in Vietnam.

Mike and I learned, with the assistance of a volunteer, how to look up and locate a name on the wall. The Vietnam Memorial has the names listed in chronological order by date of loss and listed alphabetically with a section number plus E (east) or W (west) and line number listing the names. Within no time we found the 13 platoon brothers, our fallen, that the enemy killed while serving with First Platoon. Although I said their names every day, it felt different reading their names out loud, surrounded by strangers. It was an emotional day for Mike and me. The ride back home was quiet. After supper and several Jim Beam and Cokes, Mike and his family left for the hotel to get to bed before an early-morning departure.

It was after visiting with Mike that I came up with the idea to visit Bill Davenport and Chuck Council. Bill lived in Longview, Washington, and Chuck lived in Portland, Oregon; they were only 50 miles from each other. I would fly with Nathan and Bryan in the summer of 1986 to take them to visit their mother in Portland and thought this a great opportunity to have a mini-reunion.

I called Mike and told him my idea to hold a reunion in Portland, and he agreed and said he would come. Carol said we could use her house for the reunion. I contacted Bill and Chuck, and they agreed to attend. So it was set for the four of us to meet.

I believe it was July 1986 that I flew with Nathan and Bryan to Portland; Carol had them during the summer months. She picked us up at the airport and drove to her house to wait for Mike, Chuck, and Bill. Carol left not long after we arrived, leaving the house to us. The house was a large, two-story frame house on a manicured lot and had plenty of room for the four of us. Everyone arrived at a different time for the reunion but before dinner.

I hadn't seen Bill in 16 years, and he hadn't changed. But that big smile of his had faded somewhat. I saw Chuck at the last Hill 4–11 reunion in St. Louis. The four of us had a great time talking about what we were doing now and our future plans. I learned that Chuck owned a tavern/restaurant, Bill was an Emergency Medical Technician (EMT), and Mike still worked for the state of Michigan. Sometimes the conversation drifted to Vietnam, but, when it did, it was mostly the good times we had together. We ate, drank, and visited for two days. On the second day, Chuck drove us to the Portland Vietnam Memorial, which was under construction. As I looked at where they were building the monument, I said the names to myself of our 13 fallen: Tufts, Ramos, Reynolds, Ofstedahl, Swindle, Wellman, Ponce, Mitchell, Anderson, Carey, Morris, Kidwell, and Matson.

Figure 7–5 Left to Right—Chuck Council and Bill Davenport at the unfinished Portland Vietnam Memorial site, July 1986. Photographer Glyn Haynie.

Chuck Council arrived at First Platoon April 1969 at 23 years old. He was older than most of us—hence his nickname, "Pops." Even though we were never in the same squad, Chuck and I became friends. Chuck was older and had gone to college. I looked up to Chuck because he listened to you and gave good advice. He was outspoken about the war, staying pissed at America, the Army, and anyone else who had something to do with us going to war. I couldn't blame him. With that said, he always smiled, and his eyes had a twinkle of happiness when he was around the platoon.

While in Vietnam, Bill Davenport was unmarried, from Longview, Washington. It didn't take him long to prove himself to the squad and platoon. He always had the biggest smile on his face. Bill was fun and always made you smile and laugh. He had a great sense of humor. It took no time for us to develop a friendship.

The last morning, we got up and shared breakfast together and then picked up the house. Carol came back that morning by the time we'd finished the breakfast dishes to get Bryan and Nathan. We all said our goodbyes, promising to stay in touch more often. Carol took me to the airport for my flight, and Bill took Mike to the train station. I wouldn't see Bill again. He died in 2011, and it would be four years before I'd see Mike and Chuck again. As before, I let life get in the way.

TIME TO MOVE

The Department of the Army selected me as an alternate for the United States Army Sergeants Major Academy (USASMA), Fort Bliss, Texas, in the summer of 1986 for the class starting in January 1987. The Army selected the top four percent of NCOs to attend the Academy to become eligible for promotion to the Sergeant Major rank. I had no wish to attend the Academy because I had more than 18 years in the Army, and I knew that I wanted to retire at 20 years. As my luck had it, I received notification in November 1986 for me to attend the Academy and report in January 1987. This didn't give me much time, and I needed to pull David and Nathan out of school during the Christmas break.

I called the Brigade Command Sergeant Major requesting that I not attend the Academy and to let someone else go instead of me. He told me to attend or retire. I couldn't retire for another 1½ years, so I had to attend. I notified transportation and got the house packed up and everything shipped to Fort Bliss in mid-December. I would spend a couple weeks at my mother's home and visit. Wayne and Dee would come up from Montgomery, Alabama, and spend Christmas day. Wayne worked as a recruiter in the Montgomery Recruiting Station. I arranged with Paula to have John and Brooke stay at mom's during my visit, too.

I had to take and pass the APFT before reporting to the USASMA. The physical training test in the 1980s had the requirements of doing 2-minute pushups and situps, and a timed 2-mile run and semi-annual testing were mandatory. A calculation of the completed events and my age and gender determined my final score. I passed with no problems.

December 1986—I'm 36 years old, divorced, with five children and leaving for my eighth assignment in 18 years and five months.

CHAPTER 8

FORT BLISS, TEXAS

"Never forget that you're just a soldier."
—Sergeant Major of the Army Daniel A. Dailey

We left Pennsylvania two days before Christmas 1986 for the drive to Waverly Hall, Georgia. I drove a Chevrolet Astro mini-van and packed the rear cargo area high with luggage and Christmas gifts. I couldn't even see out the rear windows. David, 15 years old, sat in the front passenger seat, and Nathan, six years old, and Bryan, three years old, sat in the two captain chairs behind me and David. We had a long drive ahead of us.

Once we arrived at mother's, I got everything unloaded and the boys settled and happy seeing the family again and John and Brooke. This Christmas would be the first time I had the five kids at the same time. Being in the Army, moving, and hours worked made family life hard. Sherrie, my girlfriend of two years, arrived that afternoon. She was active-duty Army, on orders to Korea.

This Christmas day would be the best Christmas ever. Surrounded by my five kids, mother, Wayne and Dee, my sister Charlene, and Sherrie made it a special day! The kids were excited about opening presents and seeing what everyone else received. Nathan and Bryan still believed in Santa, and that made it even more special.

Figure 8–1 Left to Right—John, Bryan, Brooke, me, David, and Nathan, Christmas week, 1986. Photographer Sherrie Haynie.

During my leave, I continued to work out, doing situps, pushups, and running. Within the first week of reporting to the academy, I'd take an APFT. If I'd failed, they might have sent me back to my unit or assigned me to remedial physical training. I didn't want either.

On January 12, 1987, Sherrie and I got married. We didn't decide to get married until we got to Georgia and then opted for an outdoor wedding in the park at Hamilton, Georgia, a town near where my mother lived and the county seat. We didn't plan a big event. My mother, Wayne and Dee, Charlene, David, Nathan, Bryan, and my Aunt Norma and Uncle Charles attended. The County Justice of the Peace presided over the wedding, and she made it special. When Sherrie threw the bouquet to the small group of women, my mother lunged to her right, almost knocking Charlene to the ground, and caught it. Wayne and Dee had a small reception at mother's house after the ceremony. I was a lucky man. I didn't think she would marry a man with five children—not to mention that three of the five children lived with me. She had never been married before, and I didn't have a good track record, with two unsuccessful marriages. Despite my earlier marriages, ours has lasted for 31 years so far and still counting. On January 14, 1987, Sherrie left for Korea for a one-year tour, and I'd leave for Fort Bliss, Texas, in two days, on January 16, 1987.

GOING TO FORT BLISS

We were ready for the trip with the car loaded with luggage and my three sons in their seats. Now I could see out the rear windows because there were no Christmas gifts this trip. On January 16, we started our 1,390-mile drive. Fort Bliss, in western Texas, was the home of the Air Defense Artillery (ADA) and conducted Basic Training and Advanced Individual Training (AIT) for ADA trainees in El Paso, Texas, with a portion of Fort Bliss in New Mexico. The Army had named the fort in honor of Lieutenant Colonel William Bliss, who was the son-in-law of President Zachary Taylor. We left mother's house and drove to Montgomery, Alabama, about 100 miles away, to spend another day with Wayne and Dee. We would drive by their home on our way to Fort Bliss, so it was not out of the way of the planned route.

Early the next morning, we left Montgomery, driving west along US 80, a two-lane, sometimes four-lane, highway to Interstate 20. We were 30 miles out of Montgomery when we had a flat tire, and there was nothing in sight; it was an isolated spot on the highway. I pulled the van off the road and got out. David did, too, so he could help. I told Nathan and Bryan to stay in the van. As I removed the jack and tools, an old pickup, sitting high in the air, pulled in behind us. I could see two rough-looking, camouflage-wearing, bearded Alabama boys in the cab and two rifles in the gun rack hanging on the back window. I told David to get into the van and stay with Nathan and Bryan. I mentally prepared for an argument from him, but he did as I asked. I picked up the jack and tire iron, making sure I had the tire iron in my right hand, as if ready to change the tire, or if I needed a weapon.

The two sat talking. After two minutes both got out of the truck, walked toward me, and stopped six feet in front of me.

The driver, the larger of the two, asked while smiling, "Do you need help?" Then he tilted his head and spat tobacco juice out of the side of his mouth.

"Thanks. I'm only changing a flat tire and think I can manage," I replied, still gripping the tools.

The passenger walked up and extended his hand toward the jack and said, "Give me the jack—we'll change it for you."

For some unknown reason, I trusted the two. He took the jack from my left hand and headed for the flat tire. The driver asked for the tire iron, and I handed it to him. He jacked up the left rear until the tire rose higher than the pavement. Using the tire iron, he removed the tire, picked up the spare, a small replacement spare tire, and placed it onto the screws. He tightened the nuts, and his friend lowered the jack. They had the tire changed in minutes, and it would have taken me and David a half-hour or more.

I thanked them both for stopping and helping. I offered them $20 for their time and help. The driver said, "No, thank you" and that they were glad to help. These two young men had impressed me, and, because I'd thought the worst, I felt embarrassed. True southern hospitality! We said our goodbyes, and I headed to the next town to get a new regular-sized tire for the trip. Of course, I got ripped off by the only tire dealer in the small town.

We were on Interstate 20 heading west, toward Abilene, Texas. We came upon traffic that had stopped on the Interstate, and there were Highway Patrol officers removing barriers to the highway. They had the Interstate blocked off earlier going up a pass because of ice. Now they were reopening it as we approached the barrier. We started up the pass, and, as we drove, it looked like the end of the world, with cars and trucks everywhere not able to move. I inched up the pass and around cars and trucks going five miles an hour or less.

David had the van side door open, and even though that allowed the freezing air to flow through the van, it was the only way for him to tell me how close I was driving by the vehicles as I maneuvered around them. He would yell "Go left" or "Go right," and sometimes only inches separated the van from another car or truck. I didn't want to stop, thinking that I would get stuck, too. We took eight hours to reach Abilene; we drove around 80 miles that day. The hotels were full, so we drove to the other side of town. We were lucky; a Holiday Inn had one room left. The next morning the roads were drivable, and we drove on to Fort Bliss without incident.

On our arrival at Fort Bliss, I checked into guest housing, an Army hotel, to get a room for us to stay until we got housing. The Army had quarters for the soldiers attending the Academy. We arrived on Monday, January 19, 1987, a Federal Holiday, Martin Luther King Jr.'s Birthday, so I couldn't get anything done until Tuesday. We relaxed for the day. After dinner, David and I took Nathan and Bryan to a nearby playground so they could run off some of the pent-up energy they'd accumulated on the trip.

The next morning, the boys and I went to Biggs Field, on Fort Bliss, so I could in-process into the Academy for Class 29. I had nowhere to take them, so I brought them with me. As soon as we arrived at the Academy in-processing building, I got in line with other NCOs attending the course, with the boys standing next to me. This was my first time on an Army post and assigned to an Army unit outside of recruiting in seven years. I didn't know what to expect being a student and a father, showing up with his children to in-process without a wife. I know that, in my earlier assignments, the command would have disapproved of me for in-processing as a single parent. In no time, an NCO's wife offered to take David, and two other wives offered to watch Nathan and Bryan while I went through the in-processing. I believed word spread that I signed in without a spouse.

I'd completed three-quarters of the in-processing when the wives watching Nathan and Bryan brought them back and said they were too wild for them. I gave both boys a disapproving look, mainly for the wives, but said nothing because I knew how bored they were and eager to play. I kept them with me for the rest of the time I took to finish my processing. I had several days before starting class.

When I finished processing, I got David enrolled in high school and Nathan in first grade, and I found a daycare for Bryan—the tasks I thought the most important to get done. David and Nathan missed a week of school. I felt sorry for David for having to attend the high school in El Paso. It had a reputation as a low-academic-achieving school and was riddled with gang-related problems. This high school was our only choice. Nathan's elementary school was on Biggs Field at Fort Bliss.

We stayed in the guest house for two more days until I got housing. I believe I got special treatment for having children but no wife with me, and I appreciated the help. The quarters were 1500 square feet, three bedrooms, two bathrooms, a living room and eat-in kitchen—plenty big enough for the four of us. I had the furniture and household goods delivered, and, once the movers had unloaded everything, the four of us had the house ready in hours.

My routine at home didn't change much. I still prepared the dinner meal every night; I thought it important for the four of us to have family dinners. On Saturdays, I did the weekly laundry—it appeared that every piece of clothing in the house got worn during the week. David and I cleaned house. Having more time at home, we took bike rides together in the evenings; Bryan had a hard time keeping up. We often went to the park, and David and I would play pickup basketball games. We played well together.

STARTING THE COURSE

I started the 23-week course, and my Army career and family life continued. Sergeants Major and Master Sergeants from every service and international Sergeants Major made up the 250-person student body.

On day one, we assembled in the auditorium for an introduction to the Academy staff and course. The speaker told us many times not to get a Driving Under the Influence (DUI) violation while attending the course. Receiving a DUI meant an immediate dismissal from the Academy, and the offender received orders to a new unit in a short time. The class had two NCOs get a DUI during the course and sent to a new unit within days after receiving the DUI. This ended a career.

The Academy assigned around 15 NCOs to a group. My group leader, Master Sergeant Hall, had been designated a Subject Matter Expert (SME) and assigned as an instructor at the Academy. The SME assigned classes that we were to instruct in advance and gave us the lesson plan. Each training day, a student presented the material for a given section, and the SME sat at a rear table to observe and encourage discussion. The SME wasn't an instructor, but a facilitator. Master Sergeant Hall received a promotion to Sergeant Major during my time at the Academy.

On our first meeting, Master Sergeant Hall told me that he'd served in Charlie Company 2nd Battalion/4th Infantry Regiment in Heilbronn, Germany. He'd arrived after my departure but served with and knew Wayne. I assumed he must have checked me out to know of the unit and Wayne. We talked about the unit, and I told him about everything Wayne had accomplished during his career. Later I called Wayne to check out Master Sergeant Hall, and Wayne had nothing but good comments about him.

We changed the module, the subject being studied, about every four weeks. When changing modules, there would be a different SME facilitating that part of the course. We had an examination at the end of each module, and a grade of 70% or higher passed the module. A student could retake an examination if he received a grade lower than 70%, but if he failed a second time, the Academy released him from the course. This ended a career.

Returning to an academic environment was a hard change to make. A classmate, Joe Gonzales, and I became fast friends. We studied together for our examinations and hung out together after duty hours. Joe was single and rode a large Harley. David, Nathan, and Bryan were in awe of him, and they enjoyed his visits. We got along well and helped each other graduate from the course.

The Academy had a requirement for students to take and pass two college courses while attending the Academy. I didn't have any college when I reported. I took English 101 and then English 102 while in the course. A professor from Park College taught the courses. Taking college courses renewed an interest in furthering my education, and I'd continue taking college courses at night, earning several college degrees.

It was in my English 101 course that I ran into an old acquaintance, Jon Caviani, and a classmate at the USASMA course. We first met at ANOCC in September 1975 and got along well, but we were not close friends. He was a Special Forces NCO, so our infantry assignments didn't cross paths. Jon had a great sense of humor. He was fun to be around and had many funny stories about missions he'd taken part in while serving with Special Forces units. Jon stood out from his peers as a Medal of Honor recipient, but the Jon I knew was a very humble person. Years later, while watching the national news one evening, I learned that Jon Caviani died July 29, 2014, at a young age of 70. It is customary for the national news media to announce when a Medal of Honor recipient died to show the well-deserved respect and gratitude to the service member who was awarded the nation's highest military decoration for valor in an action against an enemy force.

We had physical training every Monday, Wednesday, and Friday morning, in which we did calisthenics and ran two to four miles. El Paso's elevation was 3,740 feet, much higher than earlier assignment locations and had pollen that clogged my lungs. The elevation and pollen affected my breathing, and I ran my slowest times in the Army while assigned to Fort Bliss. I don't believe I ever adjusted to the elevation or the pollen. We took the APFT the first week of training and again before we graduated. If I failed, I couldn't graduate. I passed both APFTs.

After 23 weeks, I passed the USASMA requirements and graduated July 1987. The Academy held the ceremony in the auditorium,
and we marched across the stage when the announcer called our
name. The Commandant handed our certificate of graduation, and we
shook hands, just as in any other graduation I'd ever attended. Once
I stepped off the stage, I felt proud of my achievement in graduating
from the Academy.

Figure 8–2 My assigned group with whom I went through the USASMA course. Master Sergeant
Hall second on the first row, and Joe Gonzalez fourth on the first row from your left. Me on
the last row, fourth from your left. The picture was taken at formal dinner (Dining In), 1987.
Photographer unknown.

STAYING AT FORT BLISS

The academy Sergeant Major asked if I would stay as an SME for
my next assignment, and I immediately agreed. It took no time for me
to decide on leaving Recruiting Command. I thought the request an
honor—to stay at the Academy and work alongside the outstanding
NCOs who taught the course. The Academy work hours would be a

good change for the boys and me, and it would give me the opportunity to finish college. The boys went to visit their mother for the rest of the summer, and I flew to Korea to be with Sherrie for three weeks.

During the three weeks, we visited the Korean Folk Village at Suwon, traveling to the village by train. Being crowded into a passenger car and having passengers, strangers, pressed against my body wasn't fun. The Folk Village was educational and replicated the original Korean life, their houses, market, culture, and activities. On the train ride back to Camp Walker, conditions were the same: over-crowded.

The next weekend, Sherrie and I rode by military bus to visit the Demilitarized Zone (DMZ), a must-see when visiting Korea. An Army Command rule required soldiers to wear their uniform when visiting the DMZ. When Sherrie and I stood to leave the bus, she noticed dust on the back of my uniform and brushed it away with her hand as I waited for the line of passengers to move forward to exit the bus. The passengers behind us got quiet as they watched in amazement, as a Captain, with a different last name on her nametag, wiped the dust off the backside of a Master Sergeant. I don't believe we realized that an act of caring, from a wife, had startled several military passengers until we were off the bus. We tried not to show affection while in uniform. Our time at the DMZ reminded us how close we are to the North Koreans. And that war could happen at any time.

We visited Seoul and Taegu, the city outside Camp Walker, her post (Koreans spelled the name Daegu). While walking among the thousands of Asians on the streets and taking in the smells, I had a sense of alarm and pending danger. I kept looking for enemy soldiers, as if I were back in Vietnam. I knew it wasn't logical, but I couldn't control the warnings that flashed through my mind.

Sherrie had a Korean friend, Ms. So, and she invited us to dinner. We arrived at the restaurant and met Ms. So and her husband, Mr. Kim. We had an interesting meal. I'm not sure what I ate, and Mr. Kim and I drank many glasses of *Soju*, an alcoholic drink made from rice, wheat, and barley and produced in South Korea. I enjoyed being with Sherrie, but the three weeks passed fast, and I had to return to Fort Bliss. She would be home in six months.

Figure 8–3 I and Sherrie Haynie when I visited Sherrie in Korea, June 1987. Photographer unknown.

Once I returned from leave, I rented an apartment on the west side of El Paso. It was a longer drive but a nicer area, with better schools. We had to give up the quarters on Biggs Field for the new students arriving for Class 30. We got moved in, and I reported to work. While living in the apartment, David, age 17, went to live with his mother. I couldn't blame him because I believed he wanted more freedom, and he felt living with his mother would give him that opportunity. I would miss him.

The Academy had outgrown its outmoded facilities at Biggs Field, so the Army built a new campus. We moved into the campus halfway through my first class as an SME. It was common practice to hang awards and certificates on the wall of a SME's assigned office. It amazed me that several of my fellow NCOs commented that I "soldiered" by the awards and certificates hanging on my wall until I went into recruiting. Apparently, most NCOs didn't consider recruiting to be actual "soldiering." They didn't know how wrong they were. I had to work harder and longer as a soldier in recruiting, and I needed to personify what a soldier was in the communities where I lived and worked. I soldiered.

The new job had challenges and differed from earlier assignments, but I worked with and met excellent senior NCOs. I never experienced problems from my students. During my time at the academy, I had one student dismissed for academic reasons. It surprised me that I ran into only two NCOs going through the course with whom I'd served earlier. Both had been on Drill Sergeant duty with me.

On a Thursday afternoon, a fellow SME told me that an NCO named Jacobs, at the First Sergeant Course, had asked about me. I went across the courtyard to the First Sergeant Course and asked if Vaydon Jacobs was attending the course. The NCO said, "Yes" and gave me the classroom number where Vaydon was attending class. I ran up the stairs and walked along the hallway to the classroom. I tapped on the thick glass on the upper part of the door, and the instructor opened the door. Peering through the door opening, I greeted the instructor and asked if I could see Vaydon Jacobs. The instructor disappeared, and in seconds, a soldier came to the door. To my pleasant surprise, Vaydon walked out into the hallway. He hadn't changed, even though it had been years since we'd seen each other. We shook hands and greeted each other as if we were long-lost brothers. He said Lynda would drive up for the weekend, and I invited them both over for dinner Saturday night. During dinner, we talked about old times and people we'd served with during earlier assignments. He graduated the next weekend, and I never saw him again.

Once Sherrie came back from Korea, in January 1988, we moved to Fort Bliss, her new assignment, into family housing. We got a three-bedroom, living room, dining room, kitchen, and two-bath brick home with around 1700 square feet of living area. The house had an attached carport, which helped protect one car from the Texas sun. Nathan and Bryan would go to school on post.

I'm 38 years old, and Sherrie is back from Korea. I'm on the same assignment and getting ready for retirement.

CHAPTER 9

TIME TO RETIRE

"It is the soldier above all others, that prays for peace. For it is he that must bear the wounds and scars of war."

—Douglas MacArthur

In March 1988, I submitted my request-for-retirement application to the Department of Army. I requested March 1, 1989, as my retirement date. I had to stay six months longer than my 20 years because I had a two-year obligation after graduating from the academy, which put me past the 20-year mark. I knew I wanted to retire and wouldn't stay even if I made Sergeant Major. I had my retirement application approved by the end of April 1988. In June 1988, the Sergeant Major promotion list came out, and my name appeared on the list. I shouldn't have been eligible because of my approved retirement and orders. I guess the two systems didn't talk to each other. By my sequence number, I'd make Sergeant Major by January 1, 1989. If I accepted the promotion, I'd have another two-year obligation.

The Recruiting Command Sergeant Major visited Fort Bliss and asked me if I would take a recruiting Battalion as the Battalion Sergeant Major. I told him I had retirement orders for March 1, 1989, and wasn't eligible. He said he could cancel my retirement orders, so that wouldn't be a problem. I still didn't want to stay in the Army, so I told the Sergeant Major I wanted to retire. He handled it well, told me good luck in the next chapter of my life, and let the conversation end there.

Before signing out of my unit the last time for retirement, the Academy Command Sergeant Major requested I meet and give an out-briefing from my experiences while assigned to the academy. Any NCO leaving the academy would meet with the Command Sergeant Major for an out-briefing. I told the Sergeant Major that I thought the academics of the course weren't taken as seriously as the physical requirements, which I found to be normal in the Army. I'm not saying physical training wasn't important, because it was. But, at our level, academics should be more important than physical training. It's like the Army thought that running fast and doing extra pushups automatically made soldiers better leaders. The best example I could give was when an NCO received a grade of 70% on an examination, the academy told him, "Great job!" and he passed. But if that same NCO did the minimum on the physical training test, the academy called him a loser or quitter and recommended that he do extra physical training. The point was that the course prepared its graduates to work in high-level staff and leadership positions that required the knowledge the course provided—not to run two miles in ten minutes. I don't believe the Sergeant Major heard a word I said.

The post Command Sergeant Major made retirement-ceremony attendance mandatory. I tried hard to get out of going, but the post Command Sergeant Major said I had to attend. We had a brief rehearsal on December 15, 1988, and on December 16, 1988, the retirement ceremony. I went on terminal leave after my retirement ceremony because of the Christmas break, and I had enough leave accrued until my official retirement date. After my retirement ceremony, I would never wear a uniform again.

I called my mother and told her the date of my retirement ceremony, and she said she wouldn't miss it. I picked her up at the El Paso airport on December 14, 1988, two days before the ceremony. The first night mom was with us, we took her out for some good Mexican food, and I believe she enjoyed the meal. We sat around reminiscing about days gone by and talked about the people who had touched my life, from high school through that day. Mom and I talked about dad and how he'd missed so much in our lives by dying so early. Sherrie never met my father, and Nathan and Bryan had only a faded memory of him from the time we'd spent with him in July of 1984.

On the morning of December 16, 1988, I woke early. Before getting out of bed to get ready for my retirement ceremony, I repeated the names: "Tufts, Ramos, Reynolds, Ofstedahl, Swindle, Wellman, Ponce, Mitchell, Anderson, Carey, Morris, Kidwell, and Matson" and briefly thought of my Vietnam days. I then sprang out of bed and started my daily morning routine. I put on my Dress Green uniform for the last time. Looking in the mirror, I made sure the badges and awards were correctly placed on the uniform. I was ready.

Sherrie, mom, Nathan, and Bryan loaded into the van, and I drove to the parade-field parking lot. Sherrie took mom and the kids to the grandstands while I walked to my position on the parade field. I could see them from where I stood to wait for the other retirees to show and then gave a brief wave before the ceremony started. As I stood there, I thought of the award ceremony many years ago and standing in front of Alpha Company, when Sergeant Mike Dankert, Lieutenant John Baxter, and I received awards at the Division firebase in Chu Lai during the stand-down in November 1969 for the action on August 13, 1969. It was hard to believe that those 20 years had passed so fast.

It was a clear, cold, blustery day as I lined up in front of the grandstands on the parade field with the other NCOs who were retiring and executed commands of parade rest, attention, and present and order arms as the Sergeant Major barked the orders. The post commander walked along the line of senior NCOs who were retiring and stopped in front of each. We snapped to attention and saluted, and he returned the salute and pinned the award we'd earned on our left breast pocket. As he shook my hand, he made small talk, but I don't recall what he said. This ceremony reminded me of the day I'd entered the Army. I was a number going through the enlistment process, and a stranger had given me the Oath of Enlistment. Now I was a professional soldier shaking hands with a stranger, leaving after 20 years of service.

Figure 9-1 Me, center, shaking hands at my retirement ceremony and being awarded the Meritorious Service Medal with First Oak Leaf Cluster (2nd award), December 16, 1988. Photographer Sherrie Haynie.

After the Sergeant Major dismissed us from the formation on the parade field, I walked toward Sherrie, mom, Nathan, and Bryan with my mind spinning, wondering where the last 20 years had gone. But I thought of the future, too; being a civilian and working in the technology field excited me. My mom hugged me and told me she was proud and asked what my plans were now that I was retired. I told her that my first goal was to complete my Bachelor of Science degree in computers and then work in the technology field. And maybe someday teach at the college level. I always wanted to teach. That is what I liked about being a Drill Sergeant—teaching.

Figure 9–2 With family after Retirement Ceremony, December 16, 1988. Front row, left to right—Bryan, and Nathan. Rear row, left to right—My mother, Judy Haynie, me, and wife Sherrie Haynie. Photographer unknown.

Once we returned home, mom and Sherrie prepared lunch, and Nathan and Bryan went outside to play. I removed and hung my uniform in the bedroom closet just as I wore it that day. In a daze, I stared at the hanging uniform while the years of service flashed by as if it were a video on fast-forward. I then shut the closet door, leaving the uniform hanging in the dark, knowing I would never wear it again. I walked into the living room carrying a Jim Beam and Coke, sat in my recliner, legs elevated, and my thoughts drifted to the assignments I'd had and to those with whom I'd served before and after Vietnam.

I enjoyed being a soldier. I always said, "The Army was good to me. But I was good to the Army." I met and served with many outstanding soldiers, NCOs, and officers during my 20 years of service. Most were good soldiers and performed well in their job. They exhibited outstanding leadership traits that molded many young soldiers, including me, into performing beyond their dreams. These young soldiers became good leaders in the Army or in the job they performed outside the military. Yes, I served with poor leaders and soldiers, but they were few compared to the good people I served with during my 20 years. During my years of service after Vietnam, I never had the brotherhood as I did with my platoon in Vietnam. I missed the brotherhood.

First Platoon was my family during my year in Vietnam and every day after I returned. We of First Platoon are brothers and have a bond that cannot be explained. I thought of my platoon brothers and wondered what they were doing and, again, I thought of the fallen: "Tufts, Ramos, Reynolds, Ofstedahl, Swindle, Wellman, Ponce, Mitchell, Anderson, Carey, Morris, Kidwell, and Matson" and wondered where they would've been today if they'd lived. It wasn't fair. I had a sudden yearning to reconnect with my platoon brothers. As I sat, reclining further back, I pondered my future of not being a soldier. But I knew someday I would search for the rest of First Platoon.

I'm 38 years old, married, with five children, all born in a different state or country, and retiring after 20 years and seven months of active Army service with eight different assignments.

The End

AFTERWORD

"The soldier is the Army. No army is better than its soldiers. The soldier is also a citizen. In fact, the highest obligation and privilege of citizenship is that of bearing arms for one's country."

— GEORGE S. PATTON JR.

P eople I've met since writing *When I Turned Nineteen: A Vietnam War Memoir* often asked why I enlisted in the Army and then went on to Vietnam to fight an unpopular war. During the '60s, when I graduated from high school, parents expected one of three things: go to college or trade school, get a good-paying job, or enlist in a military service. Parents thought one of these choices a good choice, and, more often than not, this meant we left home.

I explained about growing up in a military family and being taught the importance of service to country from an early age. Most men in the Haynie family—and today, women—volunteered to serve during peace and wartime. Joining the Army was as natural as the kid next door enrolling in college or a trade school. It amazed me, that, with the number of people I talked to, including neighbors and friends, none of their family members fought in a war or served in a military service. So most people didn't understand or experience the belief of military service.

I thought ending with a brief description of the Haynie family military tradition would be fitting. I don't include the many uncles who served in World War II. As examples: Delray Herrington at Bastogne, Charles Coxon at the Battle of the Bulge, and Fred Lane at Iwo Jima. Or my dad's brother, Jack, who served in the Army National Guard in the mid-1950s.

CHARLES HANEY

Charles, my 5th great-grandfather, was born in the year 1745 in Londonderry, Ireland. He served in the American Revolutionary War in the Pennsylvania and Virginia Militia as a Private. He started drawing his $30 annual pension at the age of 84. He died in the year 1843 in Marion, North Carolina, at the age of 98. Below is part of a letter that was received by a relative who requested information about his pension from the U.S. Revolutionary War Pension and Bounty-Land Warrant Application File:

> . . . He enlisted June 1, 1776, Little York, Pennsylvania, served as private in Captains Ben Savage's and McGee's companies, Colonels McAllister's and Kennedy's Pennsylvania regiments and was discharged between Christmas and New Year's Day. He moved to Prince Edward County, Virginia, where he enlisted June 1, 1780, served as private in Captain Jesse Owens's Company, Colonels Lucas's and Downman's Virginia regiments, was in the battle of Camden, August 16, 1780, and was discharged sometime in October, following, after having served a tour of little over four months.
>
> The soldier was allowed pension on his application executed October 22, 1832, at which time he was aged eighty-four years and a resident of Burke County, North Carolina.

CHARLES HAYNIE

Charles, my 3rd great-grandfather, was born the year 1817 in Buncombe County, North Carolina. He died in the year 1867 in Asheville, North Carolina, at the age of 50. He enlisted in Company G, North Carolina 1st Cavalry Regiment Confederate Army on Jun 15, 1861, and served during the Civil War and mustered out on Dec 28, 1862. Something of interest that I found was the first Confederate soldier killed in the civil war was Henry Lawson Wyatt of the First North Carolina Regiment. No photograph available.

WILLIAM HAYNIE

William, my great-grandfather, was born on January 17, 1874, and died on March 12, 1942, in Asheville, North Carolina, at the age of 68. He served in the Army in 1898 with Company H, 2nd North Carolina Infantry Regiment when he was 24 years old, but his unit didn't deploy to fight in the Spanish-American War.

Figure 10–1 William Victor Haynie, U.S. Army, 1898, serving during the Spanish-American War. Photographer unknown.

CLARENCE HAYNIE

Clarence, my grandfather, was born on December 26, 1893, in North Carolina and died on February 5, 1966, in Black Mountain, North Carolina, at the age of 72. He served in the Army, a Corporal with the 245 PW Escort Company Army Service Corps (ASC) (prisoner escort duty on the front), and during World War I on August 4, 1918, when he turned 24 years old.

Figure 10–2 Clarence Haynie, U.S. Army, 1918 serving during World War I. Photographer unknown.

JOHN HAYNIE

John, my father, was born June 5, 1924, in Franklin, North Carolina, and died on September 9, 1984, in Center, Alabama, at the age of 60. He entered the Army on March 16, 1944, as a 19-year-old. He served in World War II, Company G 157th Infantry 45th Infantry Division and at the Battle of Anzio. He served in Vietnam, in the year 1967, with the 199th Light Infantry Brigade. He retired at the rank of Captain, after 26 years of service, in 1969. Some of his assignments were: Heidelberg, Germany, Korea, Fort McPherson, Georgia, Fort Monroe, Virginia, Orleans, France, Vietnam, and Fort Benning, Georgia.

Below is an article that I transcribed, from the *Asheville Citizen-Times* newspaper, published in 1944, which talks of an action, in Italy, that included my father.

HAYNIE GIVES ALARM, MANY JERRIES SADDER

For a little while the Thunderbirds in the little house on the hill were looking down the Jerries' throats—but only figuratively. There was no doubt in anyone's mind that the Krauts had the drop on them.

The assault Company, G, trudged along the road. Directly behind them was 200 yards of blacktop and nothing else. Then came the support companies and a few tanks.

To the right of the road was a little house on high ground. Technical Sergeant Gene Thompson had set up a cannon Company Observation Post there, and Staff Sergeant Paddy Williams, Durham, North Carolina, was up there looking around for the mortars. Sergeant Louis Wims, Attleboro, Massachusetts, and Private John W. Haynie, Asheville, North Carolina, went up to help.

One of the four men spotted a couple of figures coming around the bend of the hill below them. No one was quite sure if they were German, but the suspense didn't last long. Around the bend came about 50 more figures, and there was no mistaking them this time. They were Krauts.

They headed for the open stretch of blacktop, intending to cut off Company G from the support that followed. A few of them stopped long enough to set up a mortar.

The four Thunderbirds looked down at the Germans. The 50-odd Germans looked back up at the Thunderbirds.

Then Private Haynie made a dash. Across open terrain, under the observation of all the approaching Krauts, he sped to warn the companies coming up.

He made it. His information was relayed to our mortars and machine guns, and the Germans were pinned down before they could get off more than a couple of rounds of mortar ammo. Later, when Company A cleaned up the sector, over 70 prisoners were taken.

Figure 10–3 Private John W. Haynie, age 19, May 1944, before leaving for WWII. Photographer unknown.

Figure 10–4 Captain John W. Haynie, age 43, in Vietnam, 1967 with the 199th Light Infantry Brigade. He was the Brigade AG officer. Photographer unknown.

WAYNE HAYNIE

Wayne, my brother, served in the Army for 20 years and retired at the rank of Sergeant First Class, November 1989. He came out on the E8 promotion list and wore the rank of First Sergeant but decided not to stay in the Army the extra two years the promotion required. Some of his assignments were: Vietnam, Korea, Fort Benning, Georgia, Heilbronn, Germany, Fort Leonard Wood, Missouri, Fort Jackson, South Carolina, and Recruiting Command.

Figure 10–5 Left to Right—General Collins and John "Wayne" Haynie receiving the Recruiter Ring Award, 1988, U.S. Army Recruiting Command. Photographer unknown.

SHERRIE HAYNIE

Sherrie, my wife, served in the Army for 20 years and retired at the rank of Major, December 1996. She received her commission to 2nd Lieutenant through the University of Tennessee ROTC program. Some of her assignments were: Fort Bragg, North Carolina, Korea (3 tours), Fort Gordon, Georgia, Fort Bliss, Texas, and Fort Leavenworth, Kansas.

Figure 10–6 Sherrie Haynie at the Korean DMZ, 1987, during my visit. Photographer Glyn Haynie.

DAVID HAYNIE

David, my oldest son, served in the Army for 20 years and retired at the rank of Sergeant Major in 2012. He rose through the ranks faster than me or any other family member and served with Special Operations in a support position. Some of his assignments were: Fort Leavenworth, Kansas, Korea, Fort Detrick, Maryland, and Fort Bragg, North Carolina. David served several short tours during the war in Iraq.

Figure 10–7 David Haynie, Department of Army Photograph, 2003.

TARIE HAYNIE

Tarie, my daughter-in-law, wife of David, served in the Army 21 years active duty and retired at the rank of Master Sergeant in 2007. Some of her assignments were: Fort Carson, Colorado, Nurenberg, Germany, Fort Eustis, Virginia, Fort Riley, Kansas, (Desert Storm) with the 1st Infantry Division, Fort Leavenworth, Kansas, Fort Bragg, North Carolina, and a short tour in Iraq with Special Operations in a support position.

Figure 10–8 Tarie Haynie, Department of Army photograph, May 2004.

NATHAN HAYNIE

Nathan, my next-to-youngest son, served in the Army for four years and held the rank of Sergeant when honorably discharged. When Nathan returned from Iraq, I pinned my father's Combat Infantry Badge (CIB) on his uniform. Some of his assignments were: Fort Bragg, North Carolina, Iraq with the 82nd Airborne Division, a short tour in Afghanistan with the 82nd Airborne Division, and Fort Lewis, Washington.

Figure 10–9 Nathan Haynie; photograph was taken April 2004 after he returned home from Iraq. Photograph by Tarie Haynie.

Figure 10–10 Me pinning my father's CIB on Nathan Haynie's uniform jacket. The photograph was taken April 2004 after he returned home from Iraq. Photograph by Tarie Haynie.

BRYAN HAYNIE

Bryan, my youngest son, served in the Army for three years and held the rank of Specialist 4th Class when honorably discharged. When Bryan returned from Afghanistan, I pinned my Combat Infantry Badge (CIB) on his uniform. Some of his assignments were: Fort Benning, Georgia, a short tour in Afghanistan with a Ranger Battalion, and Fort Lewis, Washington.

Figure 10–11 Bryan Haynie; photograph was taken April 2004 after he returned home from Afghanistan. Photograph by Tarie Haynie.

Figure 10–12 Me pinning my CIB on Bryan Haynie's uniform jacket. The photograph was taken April 2004 after he returned home from Afghanistan. Photograph by Tarie Haynie.

FOUR SOLDIERS

When our last son came home, April 2004, we met up at my mother's house in Waverly Hall, Georgia, for a three-day get-together. The boys wanted me to wear my uniform for a group photograph. I had given David my uniform many years ago, still on the same hanger as when I'd hung it in the closet the day I retired. He brought the uniform with him for our get-together, and it still fit 15 years later! All three are airborne qualified; I guess they were making up for the only course I ever quit. I am proud of my sons, and daughter, then and today.

Figure 10–13 Left to Right—Me, David, Nathan, and Bryan; photograph was taken April 2004 after three of my boys (men) returned home from Iraq and Afghanistan. Photograph by Tarie Haynie.

I found it ironic that David, Nathan, and Bryan served in combat zones, and, at one time, all three simultaneously. Sherrie and I were proud that they served but felt stressed when they went to war. I wouldn't watch or listen to the news until they came home. Now I know how my mother and father must have felt when Wayne and I went to Vietnam together.

I am proud of my service and the military tradition of my family. So far none of my grandchildren have joined a military service. Three are of military age and attending college at the time of writing this book. Maybe the end of the Haynie family military tradition has arrived.

THE FALLEN

"A hero is someone who has given his or her life
to something bigger than oneself"

—Joseph Campbell

These are the heroes of First Platoon, with a brief description of each, that I remember each day when repeating their names. It's my hope and honor to keep their memory alive. It becomes harder as each year passes and my memories of my year in Vietnam fade away. If I'd written about these men 48 years ago, I could write pages about each. Now I can write only a short paragraph. Today the media calls everyone a "hero" regardless of their action or sacrifice, and I believe it has lost its true meaning. These 13 members of First Platoon died protecting their brothers and country. They are true heroes, and those of us in First Platoon who survived came home because of their sacrifice.

I will continue to repeat the names of the Fallen of First Platoon until the day I die. I am hoping someone who reads my books will continue to repeat their names and share their memory after I am gone or am no longer able. They deserve to be remembered!

KILLED IN ACTION JUNE 14, 1969

Near midnight June 13, 1969, the enemy attacked the platoon on a hilltop with little protection while we slept. Bruce Tufts died minutes after midnight protecting his position from enemy soldiers who were tossing grenades at his position. Mike Dankert, Dennis Rowe, and Nick VanDyke were at the same position and were wounded during the attack.

Private First Class Bruce Tufts taught high school before joining the Army; he was from Mendham, New Jersey, and was 26 years old. Charlie Deppen and I referred to Bruce as a Viking because of his solid build, red hair, and beard. He was a kind man with a big heart and would give you his last drink of water. Everyone in the platoon liked and respected him. Bruce was the first platoon member I met when jumping off the helicopter the day I arrived at the platoon. And he was the first platoon member I witnessed being killed.

Figure 11–1 Warren McVey, left, and Bruce Tufts on right, holding his M79 Grenade Launcher. Photograph provided by Chuck Council.

KILLED IN ACTION JULY 14, 1969

On the night of July 14, 1969, Juan Ramos, Eldon Reynolds, Dusty Rhoades, and Ryan Okino were calling it a night and moved inside their bunker on Hill-411 when the enemy attacked. Enemy sappers killed Ramos and Reynolds while they protected their bunker and the south side of the firebase perimeter. The enemy wounded Dusty Rhoades while he attempted to keep the enemy from his position. Okino and our medic, Doc Windows, administered lifesaving first aid to Dusty during the attack.

Private First Class Juan Ramos was an old-timer, in Vietnam for five months when I arrived at the First Platoon. He was quiet, almost shy, but ready to share his experiences on surviving in Vietnam. Juan took the time to teach me the skills I needed. He was 21 years old, from Uvalde, Texas. Juan was well liked by everyone and trusted by the platoon members. If things got tough, you wanted Juan with you. Today his younger sister, Gloria Alejandro, is an honorary member of First Platoon.

Figure 11–2 Juan Ramos writing home from the Bridge, May 1969. Photograph provided by Dusty Rhoades.

Private First Class Eldon Reynolds arrived at the platoon two weeks before being killed on Hill 4–11. He was from Weatherford, Oklahoma, 20 years old, and married to Donita. I didn't know him well because of his short time with the platoon and him being in the first squad. Dusty Rhoades and Chuck Council told me of their trust of Eldon and how he was fitting in with the squad.

Figure 11–3 Eldon Reynolds, Basic Training photograph. A photograph of him in Vietnam can't be found.

KILLED IN ACTION AUGUST 13, 1969

Moving through the fields and hedgerows on August 13, 1969, the point man engaged several NVA soldiers. Jerry Ofstedahl, SSG Robert Swindle, and Richard Wellman moved toward the sounds of the weapons firing to locate the enemy positions. A large enemy force in a well-concealed ambush opened fire, with AK-47s, Rocket-Propelled Grenades (RPG), and a 51 caliber machine gun, on the platoon, killing Ofstedahl, Swindle, and Wellman in seconds. The enemy wounded Frank Brown as he moved toward the sound of the weapons firing. Mike Dankert and a medic administered lifesaving first aid to Frank Brown during the attack.

Figure 11–4 Nick VanDyke on left (Wounded in Action June 14, 1969) and Jerry Ofstedahl on right, taking a break. Photograph provided by Bruce Nugent.

Specialist 4th Class Jerry Ofstedahl, from Napa, California, was the squad leader for the second squad. Jerry had arrived at the platoon December 1968, which made him an old-timer with experience. He'd married Claire, his longtime girlfriend, while on Rest and Recuperation (R & R) to Tokyo, Japan, the month before; he had no children. I found Jerry to be an outstanding leader, someone I wanted to emulate. He always shared his experiences and knowledge to help us survive our year in Vietnam and treated the squad members without favoritism.

Staff Sergeant Robert Swindle was from Fort Lauderdale, Florida. He was married to Celsa and had a son. Staff Sergeant Swindle, a career soldier, had arrived at the platoon in June 1969 and was assigned as the platoon sergeant. His assignment to Vietnam was in February 1969, but

I'm not sure what his first job was. I didn't know him personally but respected him as our platoon sergeant. He was aloof but maintained a professional relationship and didn't socialize with the members of the platoon. He was a caring leader and always looked out for our welfare and safety. Swindle had my respect because it wasn't often a career noncommissioned officer was assigned to the platoon or Company.

Figure 11–5 SSG Robert Swindle after getting resupplied, in the hills off Highway 1. Photograph provided by John Baxter.

Private First Class Richard Wellman, was from Gastonia, North Carolina, and had a Southern drawl. That's how he got the nickname "Rebel." He was 20 and had married his wife, Deborah, before coming to Vietnam. He'd received his assignment to the platoon March 1969. Rebel was quiet but always willing to speak if you engaged him in conversation. He proved himself during his first six months while in the first squad and was assigned as the platoon sergeant Radio Telephone Operator (RTO) after Terry Daron left for a rear job. Rebel was well liked and trusted by the men of First Platoon.

Figure 11–6 Richard "Rebel" Wellman. A photograph he had taken and sent to his family while in Vietnam. Photograph provided by Brenda Jones (Rebel's sister).

KILLED IN ACTION AUGUST 15, 1969

It was early afternoon, August 15, 1969, as the platoon moved through the rice paddies and then a large field toward the river, east of Hill 4–11, in search of the large NVA force that had attacked the platoon earlier when the enemy detonated a 250-pound bomb. The explosion killed Paul Ponce, Joe Mitchell, James Anderson, and Danny Carey, and wounded seven other platoon members. It took several hours to get the wounded and dead removed from the battlefield and flown back to the division firebase hospital. The wounded were: Ryan Okino, Charlie Deppen, Tommy Thompson, Mike Dankert, Glyn Haynie, Bill Davenport, and Ray Hamilton.

Figure 11–7 Paul Ponce at Duc Pho, Brigade Firebase, on left, with Leslie Pressley on right. Photograph provided by Leslie Pressley.

Specialist 4th Class Paul Ponce, from Santa Clara, California, had arrived at the platoon in November 1968. He and his wife, Juanita, had no children. Paul was always friendly and talkative, and he would give you the shirt off his back if you needed it. It was one hot day in May, while we walked along Highway 1, that Paul bought and gave me my good luck charm, the peace sign. He'd gone to Hawaii on R & R to meet his wife and was a happy man upon his return to the squad. I learned in February 2016 while talking with a niece that Paul had a son conceived while on R & R.

Specialist 4th Class Joe Mitchell, the first squad leader, was from Chicago, Illinois. Joe had arrived at the platoon November 1968, which made him an old-timer with experience. He and his wife, Barbara, had no children. Joe was always friendly, talkative, and willing to share his experiences and knowledge with the squad members. We were never close, but he taught me a great deal while I was at first squad.

Figure 11–8 Joe Mitchell in the center, Maurice Harrington on his right, and Mike Stout on his left on Firebase Debbie. Photograph provided by Dennis Stout.

Private First Class James Anderson, 20, was from Smiths Grove, Kentucky and had a southern drawl. He was one of the newer guys, an FNG, with the squad for only two weeks, having arrived at the platoon the end of July 1969. James married Janice before coming to Vietnam and had no children. James was quiet but always paid attention to his surroundings, and you could tell he tried to learn as much as possible by watching others. He was adapting to Vietnam and fitting in with the second squad.

Figure 11–9 James Anderson, Basic Training photograph. A photograph of him in Vietnam can't be found.

Private First Class Danny Carey, 20, from Utica, Illinois, was unmarried. Danny liked to kid around and laugh. He found the good in any circumstance. It was great that we had someone with his disposition in the second squad. He'd arrived at the platoon the end of June 1969 and was with us when we built the Hill. Danny was an asset to the squad, and we could count on him during the hard times. Danny's hometown, Utica, dedicated a park in his name, the Danny Carey Memorial Park.

Figure 11–10 Danny Carey, Basic Training photograph. A photograph of him in Vietnam can't be found.

KILLED IN ACTION JANUARY 14, 1970

The platoon was patrolling in the mountains west of Hill 4–11 and, on January 14, 1970, walked into an NVA ambush of a sizeable force. Within minutes, the enemy killed Gary Morris and Roger Kidwell while they protected their platoon members from the incoming fire of small arms and RPGs. During the exchange of deadly fire, the enemy wounded Peter Zink and Bill Davenport. Cliff Sivadge attended to the wounds of Zink, and then the dust-off picked up both Zink and Davenport for the flight to the division firebase hospital.

Specialist 4th Class Garry Morris joined the first squad and platoon around August 11, 1969. I didn't get to know Gary as well as other platoon members because his assignment was the first squad. He came across as likable and appeared to be fitting in with his squad. I know his squad members trusted him, and he was a soldier you wanted next to you in a firefight. He was from Lancaster, Ohio, and 21 years old.

Figure 11–11 Garry Morris's headstone. No photograph can be found of Gary.

Private First Class Roger Kidwell arrived at the first platoon the end of December 1969. I left the platoon before he arrived and didn't know him. Although he was with the platoon for only a couple of weeks, the platoon members told me he was a good soldier and trusted by his squad. He was married, from Front Royal, Virginia, and 20 years old.

Figure 11–12 Roger Kidwell's headstone. No photograph can be found of Roger.

KILLED IN ACTION MARCH 15, 1970

The platoon was on top of a ridge, high in the mountains, west of Hill 4–11, on March 15, 1970, and was preparing their positions for the night. Several NVA soldiers walking along the trail which ran through

Figure 11–13 Willmer Matson, Basic Training photograph. A photograph of him in Vietnam can't be found.

the platoon position saw the platoon first and opened fire with AK-47s, killing Willie before anyone could react.

Private First Class Willie Matson came to the platoon in October 1969, and my memory wasn't as good after August 1969. I remember him as a kind person and that he wanted to serve his country. He fit in well with the First Platoon and was a soldier who could be trusted.

To learn more about First Platoon and the Fallen of First Platoon, read *When I Turned Nineteen: A Vietnam War Memoir.*

POSTSCRIPT
THE VIETNAM WAR DOCUMENTARY

*"I do not believe that the men who served in uniform in Vietnam
have been given the credit they deserve. It was a difficult war
against an unorthodox enemy."*

—General William Westmoreland

In August 2017, I learned that *The Vietnam War*, a documentary produced by Ken Burns and Lynn Novick, would air on the Public Broadcasting System (PBS), September 17, 2017, for two weeks, and I knew I wanted to watch it. It would be an investment of time—10 parts and 18 hours. It aired nine months after the publication of my book *When I Turned Nineteen: A Vietnam War Memoir.* I wanted to see if the American soldiers and now Vietnam Veterans received the respect they deserved after 47 years. I wrote three separate opinion pieces, one before the documentary aired, one at the halfway point, and one when the documentary finished. Below are the three opinion pieces:

A VIETNAM VETERAN SPEAKS
SEPTEMBER 13, 2017

Yes, I am a Vietnam Veteran! I served a year in Vietnam as an Army infantry soldier with First Platoon Company A 3rd Battalion/1st Infantry Regiment 11th Brigade Americal (23rd) Infantry Division and served in the U.S. Army for twenty years.

I told myself over and over again I'd not get vocal about the Ken Burns and Lynn Novick documentary *The Vietnam War*. Heck, it hasn't even aired yet (starts September 17 on PBS at 7:00 PM CDT). But I watched some interviews on television and the Internet, and emotions surfaced that I didn't know existed. At first, I didn't understand why but then realized I am fearful that the American soldiers who fought the war and now the Vietnam Veterans will still not get the fair treatment or positive recognition they deserve. Will we still have to go on thinking we should be ashamed of our service?

The American public doesn't know or maybe doesn't care how the Marines, Soldiers, Airmen, and Sailors who came home from fighting a war—for the American people and our country—were sometimes abused and ignored because of their service. The politics of the war don't matter, then or in hindsight—American youth took the oath to support and defend, and that is what we did. The Greatest Generation took the same oath in World War II.

I am not saying the Baby-Boomers compare to the Greatest Generation, but I will say every soldier I served with in First Platoon was as dedicated and brave as the generation before us. They were the Greatest of Our Generation! Most didn't complain about the politics of the war or question why we were there. They endured the heat, rain, food, being dirty, hungry, and scared as hell; that's what good soldiers do.

I have three sons who served and returned from Iraq and Afghanistan. After returning, my two youngest, both infantry soldiers, asked how I processed and stored the memories of my Vietnam experiences. My only advice was that I put the memories in a box and stored it away. Probably not the best advice a father can give his sons, but that's what Vietnam Veterans did. I was even envious of my sons because of the Welcome Home they received. How sad is that!

What's even sadder, other than my petty envy, is how Vietnam Veterans greet each other. It can be anywhere . . . at the mall, a car wash, or restaurant. When two veterans, strangers, greet, they first ask each other what year they served and then shake hands, embrace, and say two words to each other: Welcome Home! If you don't see the irony in this greeting, then you don't get it. Hopefully, the documentary will clear it up for you.

I have been asked if I would do it again. My response is always "Yes"—with the men of First Platoon, the finest and bravest men you will ever meet. To all Vietnam Veterans—Welcome Home, Brothers.

OK, Ken Burns and Lynn Novick, bring on the documentary and reinforce my pride as a Vietnam Veteran!

MY THOUGHTS DURING THE HALF TIME SHOW
SEPTEMBER 23, 2017

The first five parts of *The Vietnam War*, a documentary by Ken Burns and Lynn Novick, aired Sunday through Thursday this past week. Each evening at 7 PM, I settled into my recliner to watch the PBS channel, wanting to see if the documentary gives the soldiers who fought in Vietnam, now the Vietnam Veterans, the appreciation and welcome home they so deserve.

The basics of French involvement and withdrawal from Vietnam are well-known to the American soldier. In the first couple of episodes, I learned underlying facts about the politics that led up to the war and the politics that got the United States committed to war. As I watched, it amazed me that the French people shouted disparaging remarks at their French soldiers and pelted them with rocks when they came home from war. The French government and citizens showed no appreciation for their service to country, however politically misguided. Sound familiar?

Both Presidents Kennedy and Johnson privately showed the moral compass of the right thing to do: not get involved, but they followed their political instincts instead. What shocked me most was that our president, with a few advisors, committed us to fight a war. Year after year, a president and his advisors continued to make decisions that resulted in our involvement and the deployment of increasing numbers of combat soldiers. What happened to the Declaration of War that unites and commits the country and people of America to fight a war?

Prior to the documentary's video of the mid-'60s, my memories of Vietnam played in black-and-white, incomplete and distorted. When Ken Burns showed 1966 and 1967 television footage, my memory was immediately restored to vivid color, and blank spots lost over the years were filled in. I found it very difficult to watch the firefights, the wounded, the dying, and the dead. I had to fight back tears and try to control the emerging fear I had brought home from the war and hidden away for decades. I thought I had tamed the beast, fear! I wanted to get up and leave the room. Now I knew how difficult it would be to continue watching the documentary, but I am committed to watching until the final episode has aired.

I am disturbed, actually more than disturbed, that Ken Burns and Lynn Novick are showing the faces of the American and Vietnamese soldiers wounded and dead, even worse, at the point of being killed. The media did the same during the war, showing the American people the war through an unfiltered lens. I don't say this to hide what war looks like but what about the mothers, fathers, sisters, brothers, sons, daughters, wives, and girlfriends who watch? Must they again see their loved one wounded or killed on the battlefield? Are ratings more important than respect to the soldiers on both sides of the war?

I will try to use this time to pull myself back together. I will sit in my recliner ready to watch the next five episodes, beginning Sunday at 7 PM. I know the next several episodes will be even more difficult. I'm almost ready, not really.

FINALLY THE END, BUT NOT FOR ME
OCTOBER 1, 2017

I am relieved that the documentary *The Vietnam War* has finished. I learned that the government will use a political agenda instead of its moral compass to make decisions, which may not be best for the country. It shocked me to learn the depth of the lies our government told the American people and the criminal acts committed by our government. The most important lesson learned is that we, the American people, should force any sitting president to declare war before committing combat troops. There should never be a president, with a small group of advisors, making the decision about war and/or troop commitment. Generals can't fight a political war; they need the authority to fight a war as military leaders. We need all elected politicians to stand up and convincingly state whether war is the right action or not. A president can't go to war without Congress providing the funds. It seems during Vietnam we had a weak and ineffectual Congress. Does that sound familiar?

I know many veterans were watching and talking about the documentary, but I wondered what discussion the documentary was creating in my community. When going to stores, restaurants, malls, the car wash, and doing all my other daily activities, I asked people of all ages what they thought of the documentary. I believe only one person (in my age group), out of forty or fifty random people, said he or she was watching the documentary. I guess the conversation is happening only among veterans who served and others in the Baby-Boomer generation. I found this disappointing.

Throughout the years I have fought mixed emotions about protesters and what I felt they stood for during the turbulence of the Vietnam War. I understand and believe in the right to free speech and to protest against the government. I fought for those rights and served 20 years in the Army to preserve those rights.

I tried to stay open-minded about the anti-war movement portrayed during the Ken Burns Vietnam War documentary and to understand why the protesters were so outspoken and, at times, violent. I can grasp the outspoken part but absolutely don't understand using violence to condemn the men who were fighting or had fought in Vietnam. It has continually confused me even more that protesters' hatred and violence were often directed toward the men who came home from war.

I respect the individuals who genuinely and peacefully protested the war based on their moral values or what they thought was the best course for America. The Vietnam veteran who protested the war was the most sincere protester; he understood what he was protesting. I don't respect the Vietnam veteran who protested the war because it was the popular choice and therefore offered a jumpstart to a political career. Let's not forget a famous entertainer who went to a country we were at war with expressly to encourage them. She gave North Vietnam and its army the will to continue fighting against HER countrymen. She went to Hanoi. Jane was her name. It surprised me they showed the video of Jane Fonda saying, "POWs should be tried, convicted, and executed" while in· Hanoi. I believe this speaks of her character and traitorous actions.

What about the 30,000 to 60,000 men who fled, ran, and hid in Canada to protest the war? How can anyone protest something going on in America from Canada? Was it truly a protest statement, or were they thinking of themselves and no one else? Thank you, President Ford, for allowing these brave Americans back to "our" country. I would bet that, to a man, they're now successful capitalists, enjoying the fruits from the sacrifices of servicemen and servicewomen before Vietnam, during and now. President Ford's amnesty program included 50,000 deserters; these men left their brothers on the battlefield alone, and some died because the deserter wasn't there. They, too, are enjoying America today. Let's hope one doesn't live next door and is needed in a time of crisis.

It amazed me to hear and see people in the documentary commenting that going to Canada or deserting their military unit during war was the bravest act they've ever done. I can't believe they actually believe their own statements. Part of President Ford's amnesty program required the returning deserters and draft dodgers to take an oath of allegiance. Didn't the deserter already swear an oath of allegiance when he enlisted? I believe the documentary talked more about their bravery than it did of the American soldier's bravery. The documentary barely talked about the amnesty program but gave those individuals plenty of airtime to talk about their "bravery."

One of the most disappointing segments was the depiction of American soldiers' drug use and racial intolerance from 1971 and later, as if this was the fault of the military and war. In the early '70s, the Army stationed me in Germany with an infantry battalion, and we had the same problems. I believe this to be in direct correlation to the "peace" movement and universities. I believe many universities taught (either directly or indirectly) our youth that doing drugs and demonstrating disobedience to authority were the norms. It wasn't happening only in Vietnam and Germany; it was happening in the units stationed in Korea, too. Of course, the "peace" movement need not take responsibility for actions that may put them in a negative perspective, nor did the documentary show them in a less-than-positive light compared to the American soldier.

As stated earlier, I have learned from the documentary. However, I am saddened that the American soldier wasn't portrayed in the same positive manner as the soldiers who fought wars before Vietnam. The soldiers didn't decide to go to war; our government did. America called its youth to serve, and they served with honor and bravery. Most soldiers never committed an atrocity against a civilian or soldier, but the documentary and John Kerry (his were unauthenticated, secondhand accounts) told us otherwise. The documentary didn't give the respect the American fighting men and women had earned. For all Vietnam veterans, I am disappointed.

ABOUT THE AUTHOR

After retiring from the Army, Haynie earned an AAS degree in Management, a BS degree in Computer Information Systems, and an MA degree in Computer Resources and Information Systems. He worked as a software engineer/project manager for eight years before teaching at Park University as a full-time instructor. Haynie continued as an adjunct instructor for thirteen more years. He also worked as an adjunct instructor for the Graduate program at Saint Edwards University for one year.

Figure 12 Glyn Haynie. Photograph by Shannon Prothro Photography.

Glyn Haynie and his wife of 31 years, Sherrie, currently reside in Texas. They have five children, fourteen grandchildren, and three great-grandchildren. Three of their sons have served combat tours in either Iraq or Afghanistan. This is a family where service to their country is a family tradition.

Author's Website http://www.glynhaynie.net
Author's e-mail glyn@glynhaynie.com

I hope you enjoyed this book. Would you do me a favor?

Like all authors, I rely on online reviews, and your opinion is invaluable. Would you take a few moments now to share your assessment of my book on Amazon or any other book-review website you prefer? Your opinion will help the book marketplace become more transparent and useful to all.

Thank you very much!

Printed in Great Britain
by Amazon